MUSLIMS IN AMERICA

WHAT EVERYONE NEEDS TO KNOW

ISRAR HASAN

Bloomington, IN  Milton Keynes, UK

authorHOUSE

AuthorHouse™
1663 Liberty Drive, Suite 200
Bloomington, IN 47403
www.authorhouse.com
Phone: 1-800-839-8640

AuthorHouse™ UK Ltd.
500 Avebury Boulevard
Central Milton Keynes, MK9 2BE
www.authorhouse.co.uk
Phone: 08001974150

First published by AuthorHouse 7/25/2006

ISBN: 1-4259-4243-1 (sc)

Library of Congress Control Number: 2006904922

Printed in the United States of America
Bloomington, Indiana

This book is printed on acid-free paper.

FOREWARD

**Of knowledge, we have none, save what
You have taught us. (The Qur'an: 2:32)**

My grandson once asked me "how to resist the temptation of evils in the life of America when one has full right of freedom, opportunity and privacy". This question stunned me and resulted in the production of this brief volume. It took me more than a year to search for the problems Muslim families in different parts of the USA are facing and look for the solutions in the context of American life.

Islamic literature on the subject of Muslim minority living in a non-Muslim society is few and scarce, almost non-existent. Most of the medieval and current literature on the subject are written and designed for Muslims living in a dominant Muslim countries, or lived in a non-Muslim society as ruler and administrator. Here the case study is entirely different. Muslims living in Europe, Canada, America, China or Russia are neither ruler nor have any say in these countries local/national affairs. How to structure the life of a Muslim in such a pluralistic and indifferent society—predominantly Christian—is the subject of my discussion in question-answer format.

Some of the questions have been taken from individuals and families and some designed by the author in the context of American life. Most of the questions relate to immigrant Muslim families and their offspring, born and brought up in America. Most of the answers are the result of the author's self-study and research. Some may not like some answers. In that case the author would like to "correct him where wrong and endorse him where right". Since the author has little knowledge of the issues of indigent Muslims, like Black

Muslims or American-converts, we are missing them in this study. However, I owe my gratitude to Imam Mohammad Zakaria Badat of Islamic School of Miami who occasionally guided me on complex and debatable issues and, at times, gone through the whole write-up on such issues making useful suggestions.

References from the Holy Qur'an have been taken from the translations of Abdullah Yusuf Ali and the Holy Bible from the King James Version. The suffix of 'peace and blessings of God be upon him' after the names of the prophets and messengers are not used in this study considering that every believer recites these words spontaneous when he comes across such names in writing or hearing.

Al-Hamdo-Lillah, I complete this project by the Grace of God and dedicate it to those Muslim youths who are groping in the darkness of '*jahilliya*'(age of ignorance) and the blinding glamour of American life. Had God not given me the insight and guidance, I could not have been able to present this before you. All praise be to God, Almighty.

Israr Hasan
Miami, Florida, USA
Apr. 20, 2006
E-mail: ihasanfaq@yahoo.com

CONTENTS

INTRODUCTION

Muslim migrants, individuals and families, are facing in America and Europe such social, moral, religious and cultural problems, which are non-existent in their host countries. They are bewildered, confused and at loss to understand the course of action they should follow. To be precise in my point of view, some of the American States have passed laws permitting abortion and homosexuality (gay rights of homosexuality). Pre-marital sex and having baby born without marriage are no problem for boys and girls here. This will naturally inflict the psychology of Muslim teenage school going girls and boys, giving a boost to their sexual urge and behavior. What should a Muslim family do if the girl gets pregnant due premarital sex? Similarly, what should Muslim parents do if their teenage boys use drug, heroin or cracks with their schoolmates; OR the Muslim teenage boys and girls want to marry their non-Muslim boyfriend or girlfriend? America is a free society. Every individual has right of personal privacy. The crux of the issue is how to Islamize, at least moralize on ethical lines, the practical living problems of Muslims in the West.

It's a general mistaken view that Islam is not practicable in the USA and Europe. Contrary to that, Muslim scholars, thinkers, and jurists claim that Islam is universal; good for all places all time. There are numerous verses in the Qur'an and numerous Prophetic traditions on its universality. "We sent down the Qur'an, as a guide to mankind, also clear (signs) for guidance and judgment (between right and wrong)" (Q.2:185). "It is no less than a message for all mankind." (12:104). "Say: O Mankind! Surely I am the Messenger of God to you all" (7:158). "And We have not sent thee but as mercy to all nations."(21:107). If these Qur'anic claims are valid, there must be some way to solve the problems of the Muslims living in a pluralistic environment of countries like the USA and Europe in the present age.

At the very outset of its history Islam faced the challenges of pluralistic society. Let us see how the Qur'an addresses the issue of pluralism directly. "O mankind! We created you from a single (pair) of a male and a female, and made you into nations and tribes, that you may know each other. Verily, the most honored of you in the sight of Allah is the most righteous of you"(49:13). Several texts speak of diversity in the context of plural communities of faith. "And among His Signs is the variations in your languages and your colors: verily in that are Signs for those who know." (29:22) "We did not send a messenger except (to teach) in the language of his (own) people, in order to make (things) clear to them."(14:4). "We have prescribed a Law and a revealed road, and a way to travel. Had Allah so willed, He would have made you a single people, but to test you in what He has given you. So view with one another in good deeds, for Allah is the final goal for all of you, and it is He who will clarify for you those things about which you now argue."(5:48). All these verses presuppose the existence of communities in diversities.

Historically, in the beginning period of Islam, a small contingent of believers lived in minority for about twelve years in a pagan and idolatrous society of Arabia, now known as Saudi Arabia, much worse than the present age civilized societies. Their behavior and ways of life can be a good guide for the Muslims in discussion now. A basic knowledge of the living history of early Muslims, from the Prophet's companions up to their three generations who were true believers and knew Islam can be very helpful guide for all the Muslims in Europe and America.

However, great difference lies in the living of a Muslim in a Muslim state and living in minority in a non-Muslim secular state. Muslims in a Muslim country live and learn the faith and practices by default; but a Muslim in a non-Muslim state does not. He has to live and learn every bit of his/her faith and practices. Muslims born and brought up in Europe, America and Canada have to earn their identity with effort; they cannot have it automatic. First of all, it is important to understand the nature of differences, which a Muslim community begins to grow in a new cultural setting. A Muslim of Malaysia or Indonesia will find a great difficulty in the cultural setting of Morocco or Egypt even though all are Muslim countries. The situation becomes more complex when a Muslim from the East migrates in a cultural setting of the West. The bottom-line of the problems is a mixture of culture and religion, in my opinion. The cultural assimilation takes time, even generations. It is not yet determined what is "American Islam" and who are "American Muslims". Slowly and almost imperceptibly, the presence of Muslims amidst other communities will result in the assimilation in the long run.

Apart from assimilation with the mainstream of America, Muslims face the problems of dietary, observance of obligatory rituals at workplace, prayer time-off for Friday congregation and Eid festivals and observance of dress code for women in schools, offices and marketplaces. Although the community uses the current system of banking, insurance, loans and investments, etc. they are not happy with the system of interests in all aspects of financial transactions.

My attempt here is not to compromise Islam with the non-Islamic social phenomena, like freedom of sex, gay marriages and homosexuality, incessant use of liquor and wine, evils of free economy and curse of capitalism, and things like that. It is an attempt how to face these social evils in the light of the spirit of Islam. It is an attempt to redesign and redefine the ideals and practices of Muslim community in the West consequently benefiting all the citizens of the country, irrespective of their creed, religion and ethnicity. Most of the answers to critical questions can be viewed in the light of the objectives of Islam, the goals underlying the Shari'ah. This kind of objective-based jurisprudence emerged to solve the faith-based problems of a Muslim society in a pluralistic surrounding.

A basic question is how to interpret and define "American Islam". Most of the later Muslim jurists, including the four schools of theology, came to the conclusion that the thoughts and practices of Muslim Ummah of certain territory are the sanctions of Islamic law(shari'ah). If majority of learned and knowledgeable Muslims living in a non-Muslim society have consensus (ijma'a) on certain social issues, their opinion and decision has the sanction of Islamic Law. Various sayings of the Prophet are cited to bless this consensus of opinion, as for instance: "My people will never be unanimous in error."[1] "What Muslims agree to be good is also good in the sight of God."[2] "According to Islamic Jurisprudence, whenever unanimity is reached among the Muslim jurists of a time, this consensus has the same validity as 'a verse of the Qur'an or the most reliably proven tradition of the Prophet.'"[3] The jurists agree that a later consensus may abrogate a former one. This implies that it is permitted to disagree with a consensus since a new consensus will be reached only after a group of jurists opine against the old 'Ijma' with convincing arguments.[4] The conclusion derived from this discussion, we can safely say, whatever qualified Muslim scholars and jurists in America reach to a consensus on a certain issue can have the sanction of Shariah.

Matters relating to belief, prayers and personal purification have set rules described in the Qur'an and the Sunnah. But reasoning (ijtihad), analogy (Qiyas) and consensus of opinion (Ijma'a) developed as sources of law in matters relating to human interactions in the society in cases where the Qur'an and Sunnah were silent. "Muslim scholars had already sensed that a rift had begun to emerge between the teachings and principles of Islam and the Muslims' daily realities and practices. They sought to restore the intimate contact between Muslims and the Qur'an through studying the objectives of Islam, the goals underlying the Shari'ah. They made it clear that every ruling in Islam has a function, an aim, a cause (be it explicit or implicit), and an intention. All of these are designed to benefit human beings or to ward off harm or corruption. This kind of objective-based jurisprudence emerged to solve the faith-based problems of a Muslim society in a pluralistic surrounding."[5]

Limitation of the scope of this paper restricts me to go in detail here. Here, this brief volume is an attempt only to solve the living social problems of American Muslim community in consonance with the intent and objectives of Islam in question-answer format.

1. ABORTION: Is Abortion permissible in Islam?

On the subject of abortion one finds a wide range of opinions. According to some religious scholars of the Hanafi School of theology, abortion is permitted until the fetus is fully formed and ensoulment has occurred, which is about 120 days, according to a Hadith of the Prophet. Abortion after 120 days is permissible only if the continuation of pregnancy poses a real threat to the life of the mother. This is in accord with the general principle of Shari'ah, that of choosing the lesser of two evils.

As for other medical conditions, scholars differed a great deal on this issue. At a world conference in Cairo in late nineties, this issue became a common ground uniting Muslims with the representatives from the Vatican. In general, majority opinion seems to be that it is always preferable to bring a child to term, that abortion is unacceptable, and that after four months abortion constitutes sin as well as crime of murder.

In conclusion, we can safely say that abortion is permissible at any stage only when the life of the mother is at risk. As for any other reason, the Qur'an is clear on the subject:

> "Do not kill your children for fear of want: We shall
> provide sustenance for them as well as for you. Verily,
> the killing of them is a great sin."(17:31)

Life in Europe and America has a new feature called 'premarital pregnancy'. If it happens, God forbid, with a Muslim family it is obligatory to get the girl married, as soon as possible, with the boy concerned or any other person in the family or outside family. However, abortion is not at all advisable in such cases. (see last paragraph of Adultery).

2. ADOPTION: Can a childless couple adopt a child?

Islamic Shari'a does not allow adoption. However, to bring up an orphan child, homeless or destitute, is an act of charity, which is highly rewarded. But this must not be by way of adoption. The person who looks after an orphan/homeless/ destitute should not call him his own child. The child must retain his or her family name and must be called after his or her father. If parentage of the child is not known, he or she must be treated as a member of the family without having right of inheritance. Since adoption is not allowed altogether, the question of inheritance does not arise. If someone raises an orphan child, he can leave him/her a portion of his assets by will. As we know every person is allowed to bequeath by will up to one third of his/her property.

3. If adoption is forbidden in Islam, how did the Prophet adopt Zaid ibn Haritha as his son? Please comment:

The practice of adoption was widespread in Arab society at the advent of Islam. Zaid ibn Haritha was a young child when fighters who raided the living quarters of his tribe kidnapped him. Zaid was sold as a slave and he ended up in Makkah when he was given as a gift by her uncle to Khadeejah, who later was married to Muhammad (PBUH). Khadeejah made a gift of Zaid to her husband so that he would have a good servant. Muhammad (PBUH) adopted Zaid as his son. This all happened 13 years before Islam, long before he became a prophet. Zaid was known in Makkah and everywhere else as 'Zaid ibn Muhammad'. It was later that the verses of the Quran, which speak of adoption, were revealed. These verses make it clear that adoption is prohibited and that every adopted son or daughter must be called after his or her real father. This automatically abrogated the adoption of Zaid who reverted to his original name, Zaid ibn Haritha in compliance with Allah's orders.

"....Nor has He made your adopted sons your (real) sons; that is simply a saying of your mouth. But Allah speaks the truth, and He guides you to the (right way). Call them by (the names of) their fathers; that is more just in the sight of Allah. But if you do not know their fathers, they are your brothers-in-faith and your wards...."(33:4-5).

4. **We adopted a baby girl, orphaned by Tsunami tragedy and brought her with us here. We had to declare her as our child on adoption documentation and passport to bring her from India to the USA. Legally, the baby has to be identified with our family in all respects of her life here in USA. How far this is in line with Islamic Law?**

The above question relates to a practical problem when a family brings up an orphan or very poor child. That is the problem of mobility. If the family wants to travel, what would they do with the child in their care? In many countries, they would not be allowed to travel with the child, and many would not give the child a visa, along with the rest of the family. There are similar problems that may have repercussions for both the child and the family if he/she is not adopted properly. Legal adoption, as practiced in the USA, would put an end to these problems once and for all, because it gives the family the legal rights to make the child one of the family members belonging to that family. What is needed for the family in this case is to follow the law of the land relating to adoption but not to give the right of inheritance to the adopted child. The child will be a member of the family in all respects, except inheritance. The family is free to give one-third of their assets to the adopted child/children through execution of gift will.

5. ADULTERY: How far the Islamic Law of Punishment for Adultery is applicable in the present age?

It is stated in the Qur'an that the punishment for fornication (a sexual act between unmarried persons) and adultery (sexual unfaithfulness of a husband or wife) is 100 lashes and the enforcement of the punishment must take place in public.

"The woman and the man guilty of adultery or fornication (zina), flog each of them with a hundred stripes: let not compassion move you in their case, in a matter prescribed by Allah.....'"(24:2).

However, for such punishment to take place, the legal system in the country must be the Islamic one. Moreover, guilt must be established in accordance with Islamic requirements, which are very stringent.

In the case of adultery, proof of guilt requires either a free confession or four witnesses to testify under oath that they have seen with their own eyes the offense being committed. If witnesses are found to testify to adultery but they have not seen the offense being committed then they incur the punishment of "false accusation of adultery" which is 80 lashes and the deprivation of the right to testify in future on any matter whatsoever.

Having said that, I should add that Islamic punishments and the Islamic legal code generally might be carried out only by a government authority that is committed to the implementation of Islam as a whole. Hence, if the local government, even Muslim government, does not implement Islamic law in whole, there is no way for the victim girl's family to seek its legal execution.

If the man concerned has taken advantage of the girl and left her high and dry, the family must consider the option of marriage, which ensures least damage to the girl and her family. The less publicity given to the whole matter the better. As for the possibility of the girl marrying another man, there is no barrier to prevent that if the girl has repented to her slip and wishes to lead a virtuous life.

6. ALCOHOL: Are soft drinks like Coca-Cola, & Pepsi-Cola permissible to drink?

What Allah has forbidden is *'what intoxicates'* not a substance. We have several *Ahadees*, in addition to the Quranic texts, which make it clear that any drink that intoxicates is forbidden. The important thing is to know whether a drink intoxicates or not. The Qur'an says:

"They ask thee concerning wine and gambling. Say:
"In them is great sin, and some profit for men; but the
sin is greater than the profit." (2:219).

The Qur'anic word for wine is *'khamr'*, literally understood to mean the fermented juice of grapes and fruits, applied by analogy to all fermented liquor, and by further analogy to any intoxicating liquor or drug.

The Arabs during the period of *jahiliyyah* (period before Islam) were very fond of wine and drinking parties. Their love of wine is reflected in their language which has nearly one hundred names for it, and in their poetry, which celebrates the praises of wine, goblets, drinking parties and so on. To eradicate this evil from the society, Allah adopted a wise course of prohibiting it in measured stages. First He made it clear to them that the harm of drinking wine is greater than its benefit; next He told them not to come to *salat* (prayer) while intoxicated and finally, He revealed the verse (5:90) which prohibited it totally and decisively.

"O you who believe! Intoxicants and gambling, (dedication of) stones, and divination by arrows, are an abomination, - of Satan's handiwork: eschew such abomination, that you may prosper."

Our experience shows that no one begins to feel any intoxication after drinking any amount of Coca-cola or

Pepsi-cola. Islamic rule states that a change of substance may lead to changing its position with regard to permissibility or prohibition. In case of coca-cola and Pepsi-cola the alcohol dissolves during the chemical interaction, which results in the production of these drinks. This rule applies to all substances and all Muslim scholars universally agree it. In this connection I may mention that when any intoxicant drink is turned into vinegar as a result of a chemical process, it becomes permissible to use. The thing in which we are interested here is the end product which human being uses.

In the light of the fact that no amount of a pure cola drink produces any sign of intoxication, we conclude that such beverages as Coca-cola and Pepsi-Cola are permissible. As regards beers and other kind of liquors having a good amount of alcohol, are not permissible to consume due to their intoxicant substance. The other intoxicants and drugs like hashish, cocaine, heroine and the like products come in the category of 'forbidden' (*haram*). It is a felony in American law to drive any transport under the influence of any kind of wine, beer or other intoxicants.

7. ANNIVERSARIES: What is the Islamic viewpoint on celebrations of Birth Anniversary and Death Anniversary? Please clarify.

The Prophet (PUH) states very clearly that when a human being dies, "all his actions come to an absolute end, except in one of three ways: a continuous act of charity, a useful contribution to knowledge or a dutiful child who prays Allah for him." The first two are matters that the deceased would have done during his lifetime. The third of this, is prayer by a dutiful child. This prayer for the dead can be held at his death anniversary but should not be confined to annual anniversaries only. It should be extended to charity by helping and feeding the poor, whatever and whenever possible. Hiring professional reciters of the Qur'an is certainly not recommended. Recitation of Qur'an by friends and family and praying for the deceased is permissible.

It is important to know a basic rule in Islam. Everything is permissible unless forbidden by Allah and His Prophet. The authority to prohibit anything belongs to God alone. No one may slam a verdict of prohibition on any matter without supporting his view with clear evidence from the Qur'an or the Prophet's statements or practices.

We have nothing in the Qur'an or the Sunnah to say that celebrating of the birthday of children is forbidden. Therefore, we have to look at the action itself in order to find out whether it includes anything contrary to Islamic teaching or principles. If it does, then it will be forbidden on the basis of what it includes, not on the basis of what it is. If parents organize a birthday party for their Youngs in which children gather to have some fun, food and games, there is nothing wrong with that.

Commemorating the death anniversary of any person in a way to pray God to have mercy on those relatives who are dead and that He may forgive them all their sins, and also to read the Qur'an and pray God to credit the reward of recitation to the deceased is permissible to do this practice in an Islamic way.

8. BIRTH CONTROL: Coitus interrupts. What is the Islamic viewpoint on this issue? Please comment:

In ancient and medieval times, before the new methods of birth control were invented, people resorted to coitus interrupts in order to restrict the number of children. This is a safe method, because it does not involve the use of any substance or chemical compound. It is a simple method, which involves withdrawal before discharge. It is not highly effective, but it was in practice in those days. This method was practiced in Arabia, as well in many other places. The companions of the Prophet mentioned it to him and asked him about it. The Prophet did not forbid them, but he told them that it could not stop Allah's work. We have reports from companions of the Prophet mentioning that he was aware of their resort to contraception, but he did not forbid them.

In the light of the foregoing, we can say that using a safe and effective method of birth control is permissible, if it does not involve the use of a harmful substance.

9. Is Birth Control through sterilization forbidden or permission?

To start with, there is nothing in the Qur'an on this subject. When we look at Hadith and the practices prevalent at that time, we find several reports by companions of the Prophet saying that they used to resort to methods known to them to delay conception and they told the Prophet about them, or that he was aware of them, but he did not stop them. On the basis of these reports, contemporary scholars have given a verdict that new methods of birth control are permissible, provided that they are absolutely safe. However, this permissibility applies in individual cases.

Needless to say, proper period-break between pregnancies is perfectly acceptable from the Islamic point of view, as long as it is done through legitimate means. When sterilization of either man or woman is done for compelling health reasons, it is acceptable. Otherwise it is forbidden.

10. Family Planning thru Surgical method

I have four children and I am considering resorting to sterilization to be done to my wife. She is weak in health and also my financial situation is not as sound as to cope with the normal demands of the family.

Sterilization, which involves a surgical process, is a special case. Unlike other methods of contraception it is permanent. Preventing pregnancy by surgery is known as sterilization, which can be done on either the husband or the wife. Any surgery, from the religious point of view, may be considered permissible or recommended or discouraged or forbidden, according to the urging circumstances of health or need of the family concerned. A family may resort to contraception or surgical sterilization in order to limit the number of their children if they determine that such a thing is desirable in their particular circumstances. In normal circumstances, it is discouraged in Islam.

11. What is the Status of babies born thru fertilization?

There is a ruling which has been agreed upon by many Muslim jurists and scholars and which applies to all such techniques used in the test tube method. The ruling states that 'whatever is used strictly between a married couple to help them have a child of their own is permissible, provided that no third party is involved.' It is permissible to fertilize a woman's egg with her husband's sperm in a laboratory out of her womb and replant the fertilized egg (the fetus) in her body for rest of the pregnancy term, till she gives birth of the baby. However, it is not permissible in Islam to fertilize the egg with a sperm out of a person other than wife or husband or both. The logic behind this principle is the relationship of the baby with the biological parents. Islam is very particular in blood relationship. It does not allow any relations take precedence over the blood relation. It even did not allow the relationship of the Muslim brotherhood formed between *Muhajreen* and *Ansars* of Medina after the historical migration (*hijrah*) of the Muslims from Mecca to Medina to take preference over blood relationship. No Meccan migrants could inherit the assets and property of Medinan *Ansars* except their blood relations.

12. Delivery of pregnancy by a male Doctor
Is it permissible for a Muslim woman to have her baby delivered by a male doctor?

In normal circumstances, no. It is not permissible for a Muslim woman to reveal her body what a man is not allowed to see of her. But in circumstances, where female doctors are not available, and a male doctor well experienced attends her delivery, it is permissible. The rule is that if a woman can do the job in hand satisfactorily, resort to a man is not permissible to a Muslim patient. When only a man possesses the skill or experience required, his services can be employed within what is needed.

13. Are "rib'a" and 'interest' synonym?

Rib'a is a simple Arabic term, which means, "excess". In a financial transaction, *'rib'a'* refers to the payment of something over and above principal amount of loan. Early Muslim scholars have told us what is exactly meant by *'rib'a'*, when they said that a person would borrow some money from a lender for a specified period of time. At the end of that period he goes to the lender and asks him an extension of the loan. The extension is granted on condition that the amount he repays will be higher than the principal loaned.

No doubt that *'rib'a'* is forbidden in Islam. The following verses of the Qur'an testify it:

O you who believe! Fear Allah and give up what remains of your for *'rib'a'*, if ye are indeed believers. And if you do not, take notice of war from Allah and his Messenger: But if you repent you shall have your capital sums: Deal not unjustly, and you shall not be dealt with unjustly." (2:278-279)

Another verse: "O you who believe, do not consume your property among yourselves wrongfully, but let there be trade by mutual consent." (4:29)

The Prophet declared war on *rib'a* and those who deal in it; he pointed out its dangers to society, saying: "When *rib'a* and fornication appear in a community, the people of that community render themselves deserving of the punishment of Allah."⁶ On occasion of his last sermon to the assembled multitude from the top of Jabal al-Arafat, the Prophet announced the following words, "Usury is forbidden. The debtor shall return only the principal; and the beginning will be made with (the loans of) my uncle Abbas, son fo Abd al-Muttalib."

Prior to Islam, Judaism had prohibited usury in the Old Testament in the following words: "If thou lend money to any of My people that is poor by thee, thou shalt not be to him as an usurer, neither shall thou lay upon him usury" (Ex.22:25). As for Christianity, the Gospels of Luke read, "Give to every one man that asketh of thee; and of him that taketh away thy goods ask them not again"(Luke 6:30).

Now there emerges a conflict on the issue whether all transactions involving all forms of interest are forbidden in Islam. Perhaps an international debate amongst Muslim scholars and religious leaders on this important issue is necessary. Almost every one agrees that Islam desires the development of a fair economic and commercial system that will prevent wealth from being inactive or concentrated in the hands of a few. Instead it encourages its continuous circulation and utilization so that the whole society prospers.

Circulation and utilization of wealth presupposes an arrangement that will permit the pooling of our individual resources in some shape or form, especially in an industrialized society. Not everyone that possesses capital can become an entrepreneur, nor does everyone with commercial acumen possess enough wealth to finance all the projects he may be able to manage efficiently. Thus a way has to be found which will enable the entrepreneur to borrow funds from those who cannot put them to good use, and, most importantly, make him share the profit of this venture with the lender on an equitable basis. Now it is obvious that not everyone with money to spare can find an entrepreneur whom he can trust and who needs exactly the amount that is available for investment. This is particularly true of small savers, e.g. widows, peasants, small income earners, etc. not well versed in business matters. Therefore, it seems that a pooling center or a clearing house would need to be set up to bring together the investor and the entrepreneur, ensuring that the legitimate interests of both parties are adequately safeguarded. Without such an arrangement, it would not be possible to collect funds from small investors and make them available to those who need them, especially if this is to be done after due scrutiny and securing reasonable guarantees. This process requires financial and business expertise, which can only be provided by a group of properly qualified professionals and not by individual investors themselves.

In the system that prevails in almost all countries today, this function of pooling money at one place is provided by the banks, that secure deposits from individuals and then give loans to businessmen after due scrutiny. The bank charges interest on the money loaned and after deducting its own expenses and profit passes a share of interest to the depositors/investors. Current practices also allow for the rate of interest charged and paid out to vary according to the market conditions, and the rate does not necessarily remain fixed at a predetermined figure. Thus both the investor and the entrepreneur gain or lose as a result of the market conditions and this, perhaps, satisfies the requirement of a partnership between the borrower and the lender where the profit or loss is shared equitably.

Now the objection against the current banking system is that it is based on interest, which is forbidden in Islam. Perhaps here we need to consider the matter carefully and dispassionately and determine what is the real substance that is forbidden in Islam.

The word used in the Qur'an is *rib'a* which has not been defined but, perhaps, an insight into its meaning can be gained by examining its context. Many Muslim scholars are of the view that an essential component of *rib'a* is an exploitation of the needy borrower by a lender. If for instance, a widow or an orphan or an unemployed person is loaned money by an individual on the condition that the amount returned would be greater than the amount borrowed, then it would be an attempt to benefit from someone's misfortune and this would certainly fall within the ambit of 'riba'; but if a businessman obtains a loan to expand his business and increase his profits, surely there is no element of exploitation in requiring him to pay a charge for use of money given to him. Thus there is no suggestion of any exploitation of a borrower or a lender in such a deal. This is a simple business or commercial deal where both the borrower and the lender are subject to the vagaries of the marketplace.

All saving schemes floated by various government agencies and private financial enterprises, such as banks and investment companies also fall under business loans as the money collected is spent on profit generating development schemes and infrastructure, which, in turn, spur greater commercial activity and create more opportunities of employment. There is no question of the lender taking undue advantages of the borrower.

Another element that needs to be considered is that hardly anyone objects to renting out a house or shop on rent although the rent is a fixed amount. It may be argued that basically a building or money is various forms of the same commodity, called capital. Thus if rental of a building is permissible and does not contain an element of exploitation of the poor and the needy, why should borrowing money be otherwise.

Equating all forms of interest with 'riba' is rather not justified. Many discerning people are of the view that perhaps the nearest equivalent of 'riba' in current parlance is 'usury' where money is loaned at exorbitant rates to those in a tight corner in an effort to profit from their misfortune. They do not think that the term 'riba' can really be applied to the current form of commercial interest charged or paid out by a financial institution. Surely what we need to do is to understand the spirit and the essence of the original Qur'anic message and not put ourselves into a straight jacket of semantics.

Rib'a usually translated in English as 'Usury' is forbidden in Islam. The Oxford English Dictionary tells the meaning of 'usury' as 'an extremely high or unlawful interest'. Explaining the meaning, what is *'Rib'a* (usury) and what is *'Bae'y'* (trade), the Qur'an says:

> "Those who devour Rib'a (usury) will not stand except, as stands one whom the Satan by his touch hath driven to madness. That is because they say: 'Trade is like usury,' but Allah hath permitted trade and forbidden usury. Those who after receiving admonition from their Lord desist, shall be pardoned for the past; But those who repeat (the offence) are companions of the Fire: they will abide therein (for ever)." (2:275)

Syed Ameer Ali, explaining the meaning of *'riba'* and 'trade' says, *"Riba* or interest in kind was prohibited but legitimate profit earned on advances or loans for purposes of business or trade. No one who realizes the economic condition of Arabia can fail to appreciate the wisdom of this rule."[7]

There can be no question about the prohibition of usury in the Qura'nic text. But when we come to the definition of Usury there is room for difference of opinion. However, the Qur'an has made usury distinct from the profits earned on trade and commerce, saying "Allah has permitted trade and forbidden usury". To determine if the current economic systems (banking, investments, trade and industries and like institutions) in the present age come in the category of *'riba'* or 'trade' is a matter for scholars to analyze. An apt simile: whereas legitimate trade or industry increases the prosperity and stability of countries and nations, a system dependent on

Usury would merely encourage a race of idle capitalists and cruel blood-suckers.

In ancient Arabian practice, *rib'a* used to double the debt of borrowers who default one time on their loans and doubled it again if they default a second time. The above Qur'anic verse refers this ancient practice of 'riba'. Those opposed to interest argue that interest gives an unfair gain to the lender, who receives money without working for it, and imposes an unfair burden on the borrower, who must repay the loan and a finance charge regardless of whether borrower's money grows or suffers. They also believe that interest transfers wealth of poor to rich, promotes selfishness, and weakens community bonds.

Controversy about the use of interest-based economy continues while some believe that interest paid by government bonds and regular savings accounts does not violate the spirit of Islam. A number of Islamic banks have been created in recent years based upon mechanisms that employ borrowing and lending on a profit-loss-sharing basis, paying no interest on deposits and charging no interest on loans. Many who are motivated by social and moral well being rather than strictly financial concerns have welcomed these alternatives to conventional lending.

14. ISLAMIC BANKING: An overview

Muslim-owned banks emerged throughout the Muslim world by end of twentieth century. Modern Western-inspired interest-based banking always remained controversial for many Muslim religious leaders. The concept of commercial Islamic banking in which interest is neither charged nor paid dates to the 1920's when a group of Muslim businessmen realized that traditional means of conducting financial transactions were no longer sufficient for doing business in modern economies. In particular, Islamic banks were founded to fund trading activity. The first modern Islamic banking institutions were Farmers Credit Unions, founded in Pakistan in the 1950s and a small rural institution founded in Egypt in 1963. Islamic banking expanded in the 1970s with the founding of the Dubai Islamic Bank (1975), the Faysal Islamic Banks in Egypt and Sudan and the Kuwait Finance House (1977), the Jordan Islamic Bank (1978), and the Bahrain Islamic Bank (1978). Islamic banking then spread to Malaysia and Indonesia. Since 1970s some commercial banks in both Muslim countries and Europe have begun offering Islamic banking services.

Islamic banks charge fees for services for their accounts rather than interest. Saving accounts do not earn interest. However, the banks offer to their patrons to participate in bank investments and either earn a share of the profit on the return or suffer a portion of the losses sustained by the bank. These transactions are permissible under Islamic law. This principle of profit-sharing (*mudharabah*) is well established in Islamic Law.

Like conventional banks, Islamic banks offer current account facilities, such as checking accounts and deposit accounts, which can be accessed either by writing checks or by ATMs. International charge cards, such as Visa, are offered but are strictly debit cards rather than credit cards. Long-term credit is available through leasing and installment sales in which the customer pays a certain amount monthly and ultimately takes ownership of the item. Longer-term financing through an Islamic bank is also possible in an arrangement in which the bank serves as a partner in the business. In such a case, the bank provides funding. An Islamic bank can further enter into an equity-sharing (*musharakah*) arrangement with a company. The use of equity sharing, rather than debt financing, is considered to be a more positive means of helping developing countries carry out their long-term planning and encourage greater foreign investment.

15. Islamic Banking in the USA and Europe

The Ann Arbor (Michigan, USA)-based University Bank has created the University Islamic Financial Corporation to offer Muslims home financing, deposit accounts and Islamic mutual fund shares. "The formation of the subsidiary allows us to have a financial institution which is 100 percent in compliance with the Muslim Sharia, the legal code of the Islamic religion," bank President and Chairman Stephen Lange Ranzini told The Ann Arbor News.

The bank's Islamic deposit accounts allow Muslims to open accounts where any profits are shared rather than paid as interest. The Bank also offers a mortgage alternative loan transaction program (MALT), which replaces a traditional home loan with a redeemable lease. The bank holds the home in trust, and a homebuyer makes monthly payments to that trust. Each rent payment includes a set amount of savings, which builds the buyer's equity in the home. When the account equals the home's original purchase price, the buyer owns it.[8]

Ann Arbor is best known as the site of the main campus of the University of Michigan, USA.

The Institute of Islamic Banking and Insurance, an independent Islamic finance academic and research group in London, says that more than 250 Islamic banks around the world manage more than $200 billion.

16. What is the legal position of 'Insurance' (all kinds) in Islamic *Shari'a*?

In today's world, especially in the life-style prevalent in the advanced countries of Europe and America, insurance is one of the necessities of life. Rules regulating the insurance of life, property (real estate and vehicles of all kinds), commercial or marine merchandises, are almost same in all the advanced countries and third world countries with little variations due to customs and traditions of those countries. Briefly, an insurer buys the risk of loss or damage of life, property or merchandise for certain period of time by paying a certain amount of premium to the insurance company every month.

We now examine the permissibility or otherwise of insurance in view of Islamic Shari'ah.

One of the basic objectives of Islamic Shari'ah is to establish a clean, crime-free and socially secure society of communities. The purpose of insurance of life, property and merchandise is also to secure security, solidarity by getting compensation for loss or damage. Islam is not against covering oneself against any potential risk. Islam only opposes the means and methods prevalent in capitalistic countries like America and Europe.

In Islamic Shari'ah we find insurance for individuals against hazards and provision for assisting them to overcome disasters, which may befall them. A person who is rendered destitute due to a calamity is permitted to ask for financial help from the state or private institutions until he is fully compensated or is able to stand on his own feet again.

In my view insurance against accidents, hazards and natural calamities are closer to the Islamic principles of financial help, cooperation and compensation. The insured pays his premiums to the insurance company with the stipulation that the company would compensate him in the event of accidents, hazards and calamity with an amount, which would assist him and reduce the burden of his loss. Such a type of transaction is allowed in some Islamic schools of jurisprudence. However, as far as 'life insurance' is concerned, I don't see any reconciliation between the current systems of life insurance with the Islamic principles of business ethics.

17. Are Interests on Savings, Business Loans, Credit Card Accounts, permissible or prohibited??

All the above transactions are usually sponsored by commercial banks. These and like functions of the commercial banks need a study as to how far these functions are in consonance with or against the Islamic financial principles.

The objection against the current banking system is that it is based on interest, which is forbidden in Islam. Perhaps here we need to consider the matter carefully and dispassionately and determine what is the real substance that is forbidden in Islam.

There can be no question about the prohibition of usury in the Qura'nic text. But when we come to the definition of Usury there is room for difference of opinion. However, the Qur'an has made usury distinct from the profits earned on trade and commerce, saying, "Allah has permitted trade and forbidden usury". To determine if the current economic systems (banking, investments, trade and industries and like institutions) in the present world come in the category of *'riba'* or 'trade' is a matter for scholars to analyze. An apt simile: whereas legitimate trade or industry increases the prosperity and stability of countries and nations, a system dependent on Usury would merely encourage a race of idle capitalists and cruel blood-suckers.

18. Are the trading of Shares, Stocks, Certificate of Investment, Bonds and Debentures permissible in Islam?

Muslim scholars have divided opinion on the subject. Dr. Umer Chapra, (ex-Senior Economic Advisor for the Saudi Arabian Monetary Agency & now Economic consultant of Institute of Policy Studies, Islamabad) has explained the reasons why forward trading in shares and commodities is not permissible in Islam. The main reason, according to him, is that this type of business is undertaken on speculation and on hypothetical basis only. It is a high-risk business, which Islam does not permit.

The other group of opinion does not see anything objectionable in buying and selling of Shares, stocks, bonds and debentures provided that these relate to a business that is permissible to operate. It is not permissible, however, to own shares and stocks of a wine company, a brewery, a gambling casino, etc. because all these either sell things or services that are forbidden in Islam.

Those who argue against such kind of transactions site the example of the Prophet (pbuh) who forbade any kind of transaction that has element of uncertainty. This includes the sort of transaction in which there is no guarantee that the seller can deliver the goods for which he receives the payment.

However, Muslim jurists and scholars are divided on this issue. Those in favor of such transactions say that we cannot apply the precedents of agrarian society of the seventh century to the present world of industrial society based on science and technology. Even in Islamic jurisprudence, laws of one place and time change with the change of place and time. Most of the Muslim states and countries are, however, maintaining Stock Exchanges where trading of shares & stocks and bonds & debentures are transacted on daily basis.

19. What about Mortgage Loan in Islam? Can we buy property on mortgage loan??

Muslims living in America and Europe are bewildered by the views expressed by religious scholars in respect of buying property and small businesses on mortgage loan. Some are positive that one can buy property or business on mortgage loan from banks and financial institutions. While others suggest to better live in a rented house or rented business till one can afford buying the property or business on hard cash.

There are certain Islamic principles, which one must keep in mind when one considers question like this in the conditions that prevail in our world in general or in a certain area in particular.

First, we must remember that the purpose of Islamic legislation is to serve the interests of the community, the community of mankind in general and community of Muslims in particular. It is a rule of Islamic law that says: "Whenever people's interest happens to be, God's law will sanction it." This means that where there is no firm ruling on a particular matter, then what serves the interest of the community best is sanctioned and endorsed by God's law.

The second principle is that "necessity removes restrictions". This is subject to situations and conditions, but the principle is there. In the context of listing the prohibited foods, the Qur'an says: "But if one is compelled by necessity, neither craving (it) nor transgressing, there is no sin on him; indeed, Allah is Forgiving, Merciful"(2:173). This is repeated in four places in the Qur'an after each mention of the prohibited foods. On the basis of these and similar verses, Muslim jurists formulated the principle above mentioned.

The third principle is that the Islamic law seeks to protect in good order five major things in human life. They are: faith, life, mental discipline, family and property. Whatever necessary to preserve and protect these are essential and permissible.

Shelter is basic to human existence and it is one of the human rights every society is required to fulfill. Since Muslims are living in all types of societies, theocratic, democratic, monarchic, socialist, communist, they have to deal with their particular situations in the light of Islamic law, violating none of its principles, except what may be relaxed in an emergency, and trying to satisfy their needs for a comfortable living, which enables them to be productive in a society.

If we look at all the aspects of transactions involved in buying and selling a house in the USA and Europe by way of borrowing loans from bank or financial agency we find it totally different in nature from a 'usurious' loan, which is forbidden in Islam.

Usury is the excess amount on the principal, which a borrower has to pay to the lender in addition to the principal. This is forbidden because the lender exploits the needy situation of the borrower charging high interest and taking unwarranted profit for no effort of his own and putting the borrower and his/her family at financial risk. It is *the element of exploitation and oppression* in usury that has been forbidden in Islam.

In a house mortgage transaction, the benefit goes largely to the borrower, fulfilling one of his essential living needs. As such we cannot denounce it on the basis of being interest based. We have to look at its detailed aspect to determine where the benefit lies.

What we have to remember when we speak about usury is that it is a form of ugly exploitation of the need of a needy person in order to deprive him of anything that remains in his possession. The difference in mortgage type of transactions and usury is multisided. Mortgage buyer is benefited when he buys a property as well as when he sells the property. He is benefited in either way. There is no element of exploitation of the need of the borrower.

It is, however, preferable to buy and sell property on cash if one can afford without liability. An economy based and run on the network of interest is against the spirit of Islam. It can only be exception not a rule.

20. What is *Zakat*? What's its significance in Islam?

It is the third obligatory act after Prayers and Fasting. It is obligatory upon every Muslim to give a portion of his or her assets and wealth once a year to the needy fellow beings, a new convert to Islam, a traveler, or one involved in debts. This is called *Zakat* in Arabic, alms in English, which literally means purification of wealth. It does not only purify the wealth, it also purifies the soul, purging it of greed and teaching it generosity. The rate of these alms is 2.5% of the wealth (assets and properties) in savings for an entire year. This is levied on savings, and not on income. Zakat is levied on the savings of cash, gold, silver, merchandise, agricultural produces, investments in stocks or bonds, savings account, and all types of income generating sources. The rates of *zakat* vary for all these commodities. The rate of 2.5% is levied on cash and cash value of precious metals and merchandise. The Holy Prophet has forbidden his own family members (Hashimites) from taking *zakat*. They cannot receive zakat even they are poor and needy. They can receive gift but no zakat. They have to pay *zakat* like others in the community.

Zakat is one of the important basics of Islam. Its fundamental importance lies in the fact that it fosters the qualities of sacrifice and rids of selfishness. Allah has allowed us to acquire wealth, but only by pure and just means and without the intention to keep it for one's exclusive use. One must share his or her wealth with others. Helping others who are in need is a virtue and ignoring the poor is a sin. Charity (*sadaqah*) is enjoined not only on those believers who are wealthy and resourceful, but also on everyone who has pledged to live to please Allah. Muslims are expected to take care of the 'have-nots' irrespective of their religious affiliation: "And they feed for the love of Allah, the indigent, the orphan and captive. (Saying) 'We feed you for the sake of Allah alone: No reward do we desire from you, nor thanks." (76:8-9).

21. What is *Sadaqah* (charity)?

Sadaqah refers to all acts of charity; whether obligatory or voluntary. In an authentic Hadith, Abu Hurairah quotes the Prophet as saying: "A charity is due for every joint in each person on every day the sun comes up; to act justly between two people is a charity; to help a man with his mount, lifting him onto it or hoisting up his belongings onto it is a charity; a good word is a charity; every step you take to prayers is a charity; removing a harmful thing from the road is a charity and greeting one with a smile is charity." Similarly, *Zakat* is one of the form of *sadaqah*. The only difference between the two terms are: *zakat* is obligatory, while all other acts of *sadaqah* are voluntary.

Sadaqaha and *Zakat* are foundations of the economic well being of the Muslim community. Individual acts of worship like prayers and fasting do not bear any fruit without *sadaqah*. The Quran says: "Don't you see the one who denies the faith? Such is the one who repulses the orphans and does not encourage the feeding of the indigent. So woes to those who pray…."(107:1-4).

Allah has allowed us to acquire wealth, but only by pure and just means and without the intention to keep it for one's exclusive use. One must share his or her wealth with others in the community. In Islam helping others who are in need is a virtue and ignoring the poor and needy is a sin. About the characteristics of a believer (*momin*), Allah has stated: "And they spend out of what We have bestowed on them." (24:33). *Sadaqah* (charity) is enjoined not only on wealthy and resourceful, but also on every believers who has pledged to live to please Allah.

Furthermore, Muslims are expected to take care of the 'have-nots' irrespective of their religious affiliation: "And they feed for the love of Allah, the indigent, the orphan and the captive. (Saying) 'We feed you for the sake of Allah alone: No reward we desire from you, nor thanks. We only fear a Day of frowning and distress'...."(76:8-9).

Muslims in the USA have enjoyed the riches, but have yet to create general 'auqaf'. There are many Muslim charitable societies but most of them collect for the needs of 'back-home'. There is no doubt that there are worthy causes, as most Muslim lands are facing abject poverty, but Muslims have to come out of the limited zakat-collection mode. They enjoy plenty of God's bounties, and they must think in terms of providing for every-one's basic needs in here or out there.

22. How important is the Family Ties in Islam?

Family ties in Islam can be viewed in the context that the Prophet of Islam has given it prime importance in the life of a Muslim community. There are innumerable instances when the Prophet has given preference of the family ties over any other ties. Strong family ties are more demanding for Muslims in the American setup. Muslim immigrants and their kids, born, brought up and educated in America, can somehow protect and survive with their traditions and identity in this land only under the shadow of strong family ties. Legally, we cannot put any barrier in the life of us and our children to stop the strong tides of the incompatible cultural and evils of social life of America. The more we distance from our family ties, the more we are close to the ills and evils of the American life. Only and only family ties can help us design the moral barrier in our life and our kids' life.

The essentials of American life are entirely different from the essentials of our host countries. Most of us are born Muslim, brought up as Muslim and educated as Muslim but we chose to migrate in America, a non-Muslim country. We are Muslim by birth but American by choice. Let's be Muslim by choice as well as we are American by choice. Let's be Muslim by faith along with Muslim by birth and tradition. Let's be Muslim reborn.

We all know, Islam means complete surrender to the Will of God, as expressed in the Holy Book, the Qur'an and the Sunnah of the Prophet. Here in America we have to sacrifice many of our personal likes and dislikes for the sake of our identity survival by doing what is good for us and abstaining what is bad for us.

How important is the family ties in Islam, the following Qur'anic verses and *Ahadees* will show:

Abu Ayub al-Ansari mentioned that a Bedouin stopped the Prophet, (PUH) as he traveled and asked "What will bring me closer to paradise and further away from the Fire?" The Prophet replied, "Worship Allah and associate no other with Him. Perform *Salat*, give *zakat* and maintain good family relations." (al-Bukhari; translation by Yusuf Talal DeLorenzo; p/26).

Aisha said, "The Prophet of Allah said, "kinship is a trial from Allah. Whosoever maintains its ties will have ties with Allah and whosoever severs those ties will have them severed by Allah." Ibid; (p/29).

Jubair ibn Mutim said that he heard the Prophet, PUH, said, "A true maintainer of family ties is not one who seeks reciprocation. Rather, a maintainer of family ties is one who, if his/her ties are ignored, will continue to maintain them anyway." Ibid (p/34).

After the conquest of Mecca, *Asma*, the daughter of Abu Bakr asked the Prophet about her relationship with her mother, who was infidel and who came to see her daughter. The Prophet replied her, "Yes, connect the tie with your mother. Go and see her."

Following are the Qur'anic texts on family ties:

"Allah commands justice, doing of good, and giving to kith and kin and He forbids all indecent deeds, and evil and rebellion: He instructs you, that ye may receive admonition." (16:90)

"Blood relations among each other have closer personal ties, than (the Brotherhood of) Believers and Muhajirs". (33:6).

(Note: In the early Madinan period, there was a bond of brotherhood between its inhabitants and the Muslims who migrated. This bond was the reason for mutual inheritance between them. Once the stability of Muslim *Ummah* was established, the law of inheritance according to blood relationship was revealed.)

Then, is it to be expected of you, if ye were put in authority, that ye will do mischief in the land, and break your ties of kith and kin?(47:22)

23. DIVORCE: A review on Islamic limits and regulations

The Islamic Shari'ah has placed a number of obstacles in the ways of divorce in order to confine it within the narrowest possible limit. Divorce without lawful necessity and without first using all the other means to resolving the disputes and conflicts, is unlawful and is prohibited in Islam. Divorce is lawful, but of all the lawful things, the most detestable to God is divorce.

The Islamic Shari'a requires that the divorced woman remains in her husband's house for the duration of her *iddah* (waiting period). It is not permissible for her to move from the house, as it is likewise not permissible for her husband to evict her without a just cause. This requirement leaves the way open, during the iddah following a first or second pronouncement of divorce, for the husband to revert to his wife without the requirement of remarriage.

> "....And fear Allah, your Lord. Do not turn them out of their houses, nor shall they leave unless they commit some clear immorality; and these are the limits set by Allah. And whoever transgresses Allah's limits indeed wrongs his own soul. Thou knowest not; it may be that Allah will afterwards bring some new thing to pass."(65:1)

> "If they must separate, it should be done with dignity and kindness, without mutual abuse, injury, recrimination, or infringement of rights, Says Allah: "Either retain them in kindness or part with them in kindness..." (2:229)

When the husband has divorced his wife and the period of *iddah* is passing, he has two alternatives: either to reconcile with her honorably; that is, to return to her with the intention of living in peace and harmony, and not in order to torment or harm her; or to free her and part with her in kindness by allowing the *iddah* to expire without arguments and harsh words, and without setting aside any of their mutual rights.

In US Family Law, a marital settlement agreement spells out the terms of the divorce and the relationship between the two spouses after the divorce. These agreements usually cover property division, child custody and child plans, debt division, spousal support and any other relevant issues related to divorce.[9]

24. What happens when fault lies with man unable to conceive his woman?

I have been married for four years during which my parents-in-law have put too much pressure on me to beget children, going to the extent by forcing me to conceive through donor's sperm. We even have three frozen embryos waiting to be placed inside me for gestation. I went through too much stress and agony right from the beginning. However, the cause for my failure to conceive lies with my husband and this is clear from tests carried out on both of us. He had promised me never to divorce me, but now he is saying that he cannot refuse his parents' request to divorce me. He says that there is much pressure on him from his father threatening to disinherit him. I will be grateful for your advice.

I am not sure whether an outline of the Islamic view on the different aspects of this problem will go a long way in helping the parties to sort it out. It appears that some of the parties are not interested even to find out the Islamic view. For example, the husband's father threatens to disinherit his son if he does not divorce his wife. Islamic law does not permit any parent to disinherit an heir for any reason. The identity of the heirs and their respective shares are a matter that God Himself has determined in a very elaborate system of inheritance, which He has laid down in the Qur'an. For anyone to try to disinherit any one of his heirs is an act of aggression in God's authority.

Begetting children is also something that, we believe, its in God's hand. He says in the Qur'an: "He grants whosoever He wills female offspring, and He gives male offspring to whomever He wills; Or He may give them both male and female, and He may leave others sterile. He is All-Knowing."(42:49-50). These verses spell out very clearly the fact that the creation of human being, or any other creatures, is a matter of God's will which is free of all restrictions and influences.

I do not know whether it is wise to use the test-tube technique in this case. To determine whether the embryos that have been produced through this technique should be placed in the woman's womb for gestation is an intricate question that could be answered only after a thorough study of the case. (However, if she conceives through this method, the child is illegitimate unless both the sperms and the egg were taken from the couple themselves. The use of a third party is not acceptable).

On the question of divorce, I think my reader should review her situation with her husband and his family very carefully. From what she writes, it appears that it may be in her interest that this marriage is dissolved. However, the way she is trying to keep her marriage suggests that she has not given up on her husband yet, and that she believes that if left to themselves, she and her husband can still make their marriage successful. I can tell that this is her right to remain in her husband home if he can afford that. It is also her right to be given a chance to solve her problems in consultation with her husband, or through the appointment of two arbiters, one from her family and the other from her husband's family.

If the husband divorces my questioner, only to please his parents, without considering her rightful claims, then he could easily be guilty of injustice. It is wrong of him to do that. The Prophet (pbuh) says: "No creature may be obeyed in what constitutes disobedience to the Creator." In a Qudsi Hadith God is quoted as saying: "My servants, I have forbidden Myself injustice, and have made injustice forbidden among you. Do not be unjust to one another."

In Islam a man is considered a shepherd in his own household. He should take care of his family as a shepherd takes care of his flock. As he remembers his duty toward his parents, he should also remember that the Prophet has told us all: "Take care of your woman." Is he acting on the Prophet's advice when he divorces his wife to please his parents? Especially when he is at fault in reproduction.

25. What to do when the US Law is contrary to Islamic Law in matters relating divorce?

My daughter's husband wants to divorce her after three years of marriage. There are strong indications that he intended right from the beginning that he would use this marriage in order to secure certain benefits under US Immigration law where my daughter is a citizen. Although he actually divorced her verbally on the phone, he wants a legal divorce because it would benefit him. However, he is trying to get her to forgo what she may claim from him under US law, and he says that this is not lawful in Islam. May I ask whether she may claim what the law of the country gives her? Her circumstances make it necessary for her to get all the benefits she can. May I mention in particular that he actually forced her to forgo her $15000 dower claim, which he paid nothing of it? We do not want to get from him anything that Islam would consider unlawful. Please advise.

I cannot make a judgment on all aspects of this case without having the man's point of view. However, I give you an opinion based on the details that you have given me.

You will not be doing anything against Islam if you do not give in to his demands. If your daughter gets a judgment in an American court, which gives her any substantial benefits in marriage settlement, then what she receives is perfectly lawful for her to take. There is a rule in Islam, which says "a contract is binding to the parties thereof." That man entered into a marriage contract with your daughter on the basis of American law. Now both the parties accepted the American law as binding on them. It is binding on him now to share the responsibilities of divorce when he wants to divorce his wife for his own convenience. Another rule of Islamic law says: "Gain goes hand in hand with responsibility." The man cannot get away with having the gains that he may claim without fulfilling his responsibility.

Most states of the USA employ equitable distribution in dividing marital property. Instead of an even split, equitable distribution looks at the financial situation that each spouse will be in after termination of the marriage and divides it in a manner fair to each spouse, taking into consideration several factors. Factors considered in equitable distribution include the earning power of the spouses, separate property of the spouses, the value that one spouse contributed as the homemaker, the duration of the marriage, the age and health of the spouses, marital infidelity, and who had the children, among others.[10]

26. Divorces in the Muslim Personal Law
What is the legal position of pronouncement of divorce three times in one sitting?

All India Muslim Women's Organization are trying to reform the personal law affecting divorce to bring it in line with the rights of Muslim women in India. It goes on to speak of the abolition of a triple divorce at one sitting in countries like India, Pakistan, Sudan, Turkey, and Egypt. It then refers to certain cases where hardship has resulted, particularly to the divorced woman and her children as a result of the enforcement of the present law, which considers a triple pronouncement of divorce in one sitting as a third and final divorce.

First, according to Islamic system, a man may divorce his wife once and then be reunited with her in marriage under certain conditions. This whole process of marriage, divorce and remarriage may be done twice. If the marriage is re-established for the third time and then a third divorce takes place, then that divorce is final and no reinstatement of the marriage can be effected unless certain conditions are met. These provide for the women to get married first to another man, and after living with her second husband for some time, she gets divorced by her new husband, she may be reunited in marriage with her first husband provided that both of them think that they can make it this time.

Now if a man divorces his wife three times in one sitting, he is actually trying to override certain provisions of Islamic law, which make a remarriage possible. Many people do not realize that divorce is initiated by a single pronouncement of the word of divorce. They mistakenly believe that they have to say it three times. A man divorced his wife three times in quick succession and came to the Prophet to tell him of what he did. The Prophet was very angry. He addressed his companions saying: "Is God's book to be trifled with when I am still living among you?" He then made it clear that the triple divorce be counted as a single divorce, which meant that it was revocable. This makes it clear that such an action is forbidden.

Most people in India and Pakistan as well as in other countries take the view of the Hanafi School of thought. This view considers that a triple divorce in the same place and at the same time counts as three divorces. The scholars who share this view base their arguments on the action of Umar ibn Al-Khattab (RA) who felt that people were increasingly resorting to a triple divorce at the same time. He said: "People are precipitating something concerning which they have been given respite. It may be wise to impose it on them." That is the reason why the Prophet's companions who were alive at the time did not object to Umar's action. They took it as a punishment, which would be valid for a limited period of time.

We come now to the conclusion that if a man divorces his wife three times at the same time, he violates God's law and commits something that is forbidden. His words count as a single divorce. Revoking the divorce and reinstating the marriage requires a fresh marriage contract if the woman's waiting period (iddah) is over. Reinstating the marriage within the waiting period does not require a fresh marriage contract. In any case, it requires a minimum of two witnesses.

27. What's the waiting period of divorced woman and what about her maintenance (*nafaqah*)??

The waiting period of divorced woman differs according to circumstances and conditions applicable to the women herself. If the woman is pregnant at the time of divorce, her waiting period lasts until she has delivered her baby. If she is not pregnant, her waiting period lasts until she has completed three menstruations period or three period of cleanliness from menstruation. If she is too young and too old to have the period, the waiting period shall last for three lunar months.

As regards maintenance of divorced woman during post-divorce period, I quote the following Quranic verse:

"For divorced women maintenance (should be provided) on a reasonable scale. This is a duty on the righteous."

This verse is not referring to a legal right of maintenance, which lasts over any specified period of time. It is concerned with the alleviation of the pain of divorcees. Some jurists advocate to impose on the divorcing husband take care of divorced woman for the rest of the woman's life or until she married someone else. This is also demanded by a number of organizations concerned with women's rights in Muslim countries. That the woman should have provisions for their welfare after divorce is certainly needed. Whether this should be provided by their divorcing husbands or by their parents and relations, there are different views. What the Quranic verse is concerned here with is the absence of all injustices done to the divorced women, and the provision of a reasonable standard of living for divorced women.

That can best be achieved through the implementation of Islamic law, which makes the family of a divorced woman, i.e. her parents, brothers, or uncles, responsible for her living. If she has no family support, then the state should provide her with a decent standard of living. It does not call for shifting of responsibilities elsewhere, i.e. to the divorcing husband. It is below dignity of a woman to rely for her living on a man with whom she no longer has any legal relationship.

In US Law, if a man divorces his wife, a marital settlement agreement is executed between the two spouses. This agreement spells out the terms of the divorce and the relationship between the spouses after the divorce. This agreement usually covers property division, child custody and support, debt division, spousal support, and any other relevant issues related to the divorce.[11]

28. Why men, not women, have right to divorce?

Before answering this question, I seek to establish two points. There are certain differences in men and women, some of which are physical, and others psychological, while still others relate to the roles, which they play in life and society. Hence equality must take these differences into consideration. If we were to treat men and women without consideration to these differences, we may easily commit injustice to either sex.

The second point is that the Islamic system must be considered as it is applied to the Muslim community. In a Muslim community an individual has certain social and legal pressures to bear on his behavior and bring it, as far as possible, within the Islamic code of life.

From the Islamic point of view, marriage is a contract between two parties who are considered equal. Yet men are given a point of privilege with regard to termination of this contract. This is stated clearly in verses 228-229 of Surah 2 in the middle of a long passage on the legislation that concerns divorce.

In a Muslim family, the man must look after his wife. She needs not provide even a very small share of the family expense, although she may be better off than her husband. If the marriage breaks up, the man must provide for her during the waiting period, and pay her dower. If they have young children, he must pay for their upbringing, even though they may remain with their mother.

This shows that the man stands to incur a heavy financial obligation if the marriage breaks up. If the woman is given the same right to terminate the marriage at any moment, she cannot impose on the man the financial commitment which he may not be able to undertake and which are not allowed for in the marriage contract.

When man divorces the woman, she need not worry about her living. She goes back to her family. If she has no relatives, the state should provide her maintenance.

Yet Islam is aware that a marriage may go wrong and there may be genuine reasons for the woman to wish to terminate the marriage contract. Hence it provides a fair way for her to obtain the termination of her marriage without difficulty. She may apply for this termination known as Khula. Certain rules apply in this case, which require her to refund the dower she received from her husband at the time of marriage or forfeit her claim if she did not receive after her marriage.

What is practiced nowadays in Muslim countries may be at variance with Islamic law. There is much abuse of the law of divorce, which results from two main causes—people's life has become far removed from that envisaged by Islam, and the prevailing ignorance of their privileges and obligations under Islamic law. Hence a return to Islamic life would bring justice to all concerned.

The law regulating divorces in Europe and America are applicable to all citizens irrespective of religion, creed or gender. Husband and wife in case of divorce share the obligations and benefits equally. They become equal partner in the share of assets and properties and equal partners in debts and obligations.

29. How the rights of children are protected in divorce according to US Law and Shari'ah?

I have two children, age 6 and 1, but I am not happy with my wife due to differences of social background. I intend to marry a woman from my own small town. If my present wife asks for divorce I will grant her that, but I would like to know what are my obligations toward her and my children.

According *Shari'a*, if you divorce your wife you must keep her in your home during her waiting period, called '*iddah*' when you continue to be responsible for her maintenance. During this period you can reinstate your marriage without a need for a new marriage contract or a dower, although you need to have two witnesses. If this waiting period lapses and you have not reconciled, the divorce becomes final. Your wife will be entitled to receive any outstanding portion of her dower, as well as maintenance (*mit'ah*).

The amount of this gift is determined by the husband in accordance with his means. As for your children, your responsibility does not change toward them on account of your divorce. You remain responsible for their upbringing, maintenance and education, up to the legal age, even though they continue to live with their mother. A child of a broken family may choose to stay with the mother after such a choice is given. The father remains responsible for the living expenses, upbringing and education of the child. When the woman's waiting period is over, the man is no longer responsible for her maintenance. Her own family should look after her.

According US Law, child support is paid by the noncutodial parent, as the custodial parent's obligations and responsibilities are fulfilled by having custody of the child. This doesn't necessarily mean that a mother would not have to pay child support to a father who has custody – the mother has the same duty as the father would if he didn't have sole custody. Moreover, an unmarried father – who is acknowledged as the biological father – will also be responsible for paying child support.

Normally, child support stops when a child turns 18, unless the child is still a full-time student. If the child is a full-time student, the child support can continue until the child turns 21. The US federal government requires all states to adopt child support guidelines. The formula takes into consideration custody arrangements. Many states have child support enforcement divisions, which can help get child support by bringing actions in court to get child support orders, locating deadbeat parents and getting their income and employment information.

In matters relating to child custody, a court, in general, takes into account the best interest of the child. US courts take into account several factors, including the age and mental/physical health of the child, the lifestyle and habits of the parents, the love and emotional ties between child and parent, the mental/physical health of the parent, the child's established living pattern, the child's preference, the quality of available schools, and the ability of the parent to provide food and shelter. Most courts do not inherently favor the mother anymore, as they once did, but if both are equally suitable, the mother will often get custody.

The only difference between Islamic *Shari'a* and US Law is that the custody of the child is given only to mother in the former and to any one of the spouses in the later case.

30. Can a woman divorce her husband?

There can be innumerable conditions and situations when a wife would like to terminate her marriage contract. She can do that by way of petitioning for 'Khula' in a civil law court, requesting for the termination of her marriage. There is no doubt that the court would grant her request.

Alternatively, she should ask her husband to divorce her. If the two parties agree on that, the matter could be resolved and divorce given amicably.

Allah has given the right of divorce to the man in any marriage because it is he who bears all the financial commitments resulting from this relationship. He has to pay a dowry to his wife and provide a home for both of them and their children. He has also to support his wife financially, even if she is rich. When a man divorces his wife, he takes upon himself certain financial obligations. Apart from the payment of her dowry, he pays her maintenance during her waiting period and maintenance of child/children, if any. A woman does not pay any of these expenses. The distribution of financial responsibilities is the main reason that Islam gives the right of divorce to the man.

31. What is *Khula*?

The terminology *'khula'* is termination of marriage at a woman's request. She does not need to provide reasons other than that she is not happy with her marriage and that she is not willing to continue with her husband. There is a reference to such a situation in the Qur'an (2:229). A precedent took place at the time of the Prophet when Thabit ibn Qais's wife came to the Prophet complaining of her marital situation. She stated clearly that she had nothing to talk against her husband, neither in his manners nor in his religious attitude. She simply was not happy living with him. The Prophet asked her whether she was willing to return the garden, which Thabit had given her as dower. She said she would and the Prophet told the man to accept the garden and divorce her.

There are differences between *'khula'* and divorce. In Khula, the waiting period of the woman lasts only for one menstruation period, to make sure she is not pregnant. Second, her husband cannot reinstate marriage during her waiting period. Third, she has to payback something to her husband against the dower she had received. It is open to the man and the woman to agree on a compensation mutually agreed.

Custody for the children is given to the mother for certain age. This is conditioned that the mother would not marry during child-care. When the child reaches an age when he or she no longer needs to be looked after by the mother, he or she is given the choice to join either parent until a boy attains puberty or a girl gets married.

32. How the issue of 'Dower' solved in case of death of spouse? Could you please explain what happens to the dower if it remains unpaid until the husband dies? Could you also explain what happens to the dower if the wife dies first, without the dower being paid?

The dower is an amount of money, which may be in cash or kind or some other benefit, which is payable to the wife by the husband <u>at the time when they are married</u>; i.e. when the marriage contract is made. It may be deferred until a later date or deferred indefinitely, but it remains payable if the wife demands it at any time. When it is paid, it becomes the property of the woman. The amount of the dower which the bridegroom has to give to the bride has not been prescribed by the law. It depends entirely on the agreement of the two parties, and may consist of anything. The relevant Quranic verse is as follows:

"Give to women their marriage portions in the spirit of a gift: but if they, of their own accord, give up to you any portion of that, then enjoy it with pleasure." (4:4)

There is no fixed amount for a woman's dower. Normally the husband and his prospective wife's guardian agree upon its amount. A dower may be in cash or kind or any service to the benefit of the prospective wife. The Prophet asked one of his companions who wanted to get married, how much he could afford in dower. When he learnt that the man did not have any money, the Prophet asked him if he had learnt any parts of the Quran. When the man answered that he knew certain *surahs* (verses of the Qur'an), the Prophet sanctioned the marriage on the basis that the husband would teach his wife those *surahs*. That was her dower.

In another incident, a man called Abu Talha, a non-Muslim, proposed to a Muslim woman. She said to him: you are not one to be rejected, but since you are a non-believer, a marriage between us is impossible. If you accept Islam, I will take that as dower and will ask you nothing more. The man became a Muslim and the Prophet sanctioned the marriage.

In certain societies the dower is considered as a formality. It is specified but not paid and the bride is required to declare that she has forgone her right to it. Such a practice is unIslamic. The fixation and the payment of dower should be realistic, meaningful and acceptable to both the parties, and it is much preferable to pay it at the time of marriage contract.

In US Marriage Law there is no system of 'dower'. After a marriage is contracted, both spouses become shareholder in their assets and properties; it replaces the benefits and obligations of dower.

33. What is the Dietary Code in Islam?

On four separate occasions, the Qur'an mentions the type of animal food, which is forbidden to us. In all the four occasions the same prohibition is made clear.

"I do not find in what has been revealed to me anything which is forbidden to eat unless it be carrion or spilled blood, or the flesh of swine, for all this is an impurity, or an abomination upon which the name of someone other than Allah has been invoked. But if one is driven by utter necessity, with no intention to violate or transgress, then your Lord is mot forgiving, compassionate."(6:145)

This verse makes it absolutely clear that what is forbidden is only those four types: (i) carrion (dead animals), (ii) spilled blood; (iii) the flesh of swine and (iv) any animal, which is slaughtered with the invocation of the name of anyone other than Allah. Verse 5:3 gives further details of the above four types. These Qur'anic injunctions relate to all kinds of animals and birds that are either domesticated or wild. It is not necessary to slaughter the wild beast or bird in the same manner as domesticated animal or bird. As for sea food Allah has permitted all of it without restriction:

"Lawful to you is the pursuit of water-game and its use for food, - for the benefit of yourselves and those who travel….."(5:96)

As regards meat of the animals slaughtered by "the People of the Book" Allah says,

"This day all good and pure things are made lawful to you. The food of the People of the Book is lawful to you and yours is lawful to them….(5:5)".

Before revelation of this verse, some believers used to treat the Jews and Christians in the same manner as idolaters in matters related to food.

34. Canned meat: Is it permissible to eat the canned meat processed in the USA and Europe?

Unless we have a good reason for suspicion, we can use the canned meat of the "People of the Book" in our kitchen. As regards canned meat processed in countries other than 'People of the Book', there can be more than one opinion. Qadi Ibn al-Arabi, a Maliki jurist, in explaining the verse "The food of the People of the Book is lawful to you and yours is lawful to them"(5:5) says, "I was asked, if a Christian kills a chicken by cutting off its head and then cooks it, is it permissible to eat with him or to partake of his food? I said, 'Eat it, as this is his food and the food of his priests and monks. Although this is not our way of slaughtering the animal, yet Allah has permitted their food to us.' Our scholars have said: They give us their women in marriage and it is permissible to engage in sexual relation with them. In matters concerning *halal* and *haram* sexual relation is of graver import than eating; how then does it make sense to say that their food is not *halal*?[12]

In the light of the above study, we can safely say that meats of animals and birds originating from the People of the Book, whether canned or un-canned, are *halal* (permissible) for us even though the animal may have been slaughtered by help of electric shock or otherwise. As long as they consider it lawful in their religion, it is lawful for us.

All kosher products of Jews community are permissible for Muslims as they slaughter the animals as we do and they consider the meat of swine forbidden.

An element of doubt arise in the meat and meat products of Christian community only when one does not know whether the canned beef or mutton has been processed and packed separate from the processing and packing of pork. It is better to avoid use of such products where there is an element of doubt.

35. Are the meat of animals slaughtered by Christians and Jews permissible to eat, even though they may not slaughter their animals in the manner recommended by Islam?

Islamic Shari'a requires that the following method of slaughter be followed to sanctify the meat of the animals slaughtered: (i) The animal should be slaughtered by a sharp object (metal, stone or wood) making it bleed. (ii) Slaughtering to be done by cutting or piercing the throat of the animal causing its death. (iii) The name of Allah be mentioned with *"Bi-Ismillah Allah-o-Akbar"* at the time of slaughter. This method is further supported by other sound *ahadith*, which state that Allah's name must be pronounced while hunting just before an arrow is shot or a hunting dog is sent for the chase.

The Christians and Jews of Arabia at the time of the Prophet slaughtered their animals in the method recommended by the Bible, following the same method as Muslims. Jews still do this, but Christians have introduced new method of stunning by electric shock. However, the meat of animals slaughtered by the 'People of the Book' is permissible to eat and the same is true with chickens.

"The food of the People of the Book is lawful to you and yours is lawful to them." (Q.5:5)

This refers to their slaughtered animals. A Jewish woman brought a lamb to the Prophet and he started to eat from it before realizing that it was poisoned. He did not question her on the method of slaughter she followed.

His companions also asked him: "Meat is brought to us and we do not know if God's name has been mentioned at the time of its slaughter. What should we do?" He said: "Mention God's name and eat."[13]

However, our current discussion relates to the question of how far the meat of animals slaughtered by Jews and Christians are permissible or prohibited for Muslims in the current age. As Shari'a Law is to Muslims, the Jewish Law is to Jews. They adhere to the sanctions of Torah in their dietary practices. They slaughter their animals in the same manner as Muslims do. One of the renowned orientalists, John Esposito, writes in his book, "Dietary regulations, particularly the requirements to eat meat that has been slaughtered in a religiously appropriate way (*halal*) and not to eat pork products, are often difficult to follow in an American setting. A *halal* butcher shop may not be available, and American food manufacturers and restaurants often use pork-based products, particularly lard, to prepare food. Many Muslims who have not been able to find *halal* meat shops have turned instead to Jewish kosher butchers."[14] Pork and pork products, along with other meat products are commonly used in the American chain stores and restaurants. The Christian method of slaughter is also different to the Muslims and Jews method. There is no separate treatment in their animal husbandry, butchery and meat processing plant for raising, slaughtering and packing the pork products and *halal* products. They are all done at one place and, perhaps, using the same method and machine. It is for this reason of pork and pork products and not for the reason of method of slaughter that creates the element of doubt for Muslims to use the meat and meat products of the animals slaughtered by the Christians.

36. Muslim Students studying in Europe & America and living in hostels and dormitories; workers living in field camps and trailers; soldiers serving in the three forces of the US and Europe; staff working in healthcare hospitals and institutions and working in corporate organizations; How can such people observe the dietary principles of Islam?

In this context, after listing the prohibited foods in the form of dead animals, blood and pork, Allah says:

"....but if one is compelled by necessity, neither craving (it) nor transgressing, there is no sin on him; indeed, Allah is Forgiving, Merciful." (2:173)

This is repeated at four places in the Qur'an after each mention of the prohibited foods. On the basis of these, Islamic jurists formulated an important principle, namely, "that necessity removes restrictions."   In permitting the use of the *haram* food under necessity, Islam is true to its spirit and general principles. "Allah desires ease for you, and He does not desire hardship for you ...." (2:185). "He desires to lighten your burden, for man was created weak.(4:28)" However, the fact remains that God has mentioned specifically that the food eaten by the 'People of the Book' is lawful for Muslims to eat. He has always been aware of what methods of slaughter they would be using. Nevertheless, He has made the concession allowing us to eat their food. Hence, we say that it is permissible to eat of the meat of the animals slaughtered in the USA and Europe, unless the meat of the permissible animals is of a type, which is exclusively slaughtered, processed and packed separate from the meat of pork, which is clearly forbidden.

Anyhow if someone wants to refrain from eating such meat because they feel that certain restrictions apply to it, they have right to do as they wish. Most of the institutions in question provide Muslim meals, if and when demanded. In case there is no facility to provide Muslim meals, one can restrict to the veggies or fish food.

When there are differences between scholars, we respect those differences, and do what we feel is in line with God's wishes. In such cases, Islam does not wish to overburden its followers. God has given this concession to make it easy for Muslims who live in Europe and other non-Muslim countries. Hence we should not place the burden on ourselves, because God has not chosen to place it on us. Had He wished to make such restrictions, He would have stated them clearly. He has not, so no one may forbid what God has not made forbidden.

37. Are the meat (beef, mutton and chickens & birds of prey), available in the USA, Canada and Europe permissible to eat?

We have an indisputable Islamic juristic rule, which makes it clear that "every thing is lawful unless it is pronounced otherwise." Moreover, the authority to forbid any thing belongs solely to God. There are certain things that the Prophet specified as forbidden but he did so on God's authority. Bearing that in mind, we have to have a sound basis before we could slam a verdict of prohibition on any matter. When the Prophet told his companions and succeeding generations of his followers to mention God's name before eating meat slaughtered by non-Muslims, he was showing them the way to make certain that such meat was lawful. We do well to follow his guidance, and indeed that is all that is required of us today.

As for the Qur'anic verse, which says: "Do not eat of the meat of any (animal) on which God's name has not been invoked." In this connection, scholars mention a Hadith, which tells us that the Prophet's companions put to him the question that they might have meat but they would not know if God's name was invoked at the time of slaughter. He told them to mention God's name and eat it.

However, this is not a major point of issue. What are prohibited to eat is clearly specified in Verse 145, surah 6 of the Qur'an:

"Say: I do not find in all the revelations given to me anything that is forbidden to eat by anyone, unless it be carrion (dead animal), running blood, and the flesh of swine and any flesh that has been profanely consecrated to beings other than God."

We cannot have more definitive statement. When everything has been said and clarified, people should choose the line of action with which they feel more comfortable.

As regards the Qur'anic verse which states that "the food of the people of earlier scriptures is permissible for you to eat", there is no disagreement among scholars that this verse refers to slaughtered animals. Animals slaughtered by Christians and Jews are permissible for Muslims to eat because it is forbidden in their religions to consecrate the slaughter of any animal for any one's name other than God. This does not apply to other religions. Hence the restriction on Muslims not to eat the slaughtered animals of the followers of the religions other than People of the Book.

Allah has made it permissible for us to eat anything the earth produces with the exception of those items, which He has specifically forbidden. If we are eating vegetable or seafood dishes we need not ask who prepared it, because it does not matter from the viewpoint of Islam what religion the cook follows. What is forbidden for Muslims to eat is that which Allah has forbidden for a specific reason. He has not forbidden anything due to the identity or the faith of the person who cooks it. When something is forbidden it remains forbidden even though a Muslim may cook it.

38. DRESS CODE: What is the dress code in Islam? Does Islam forbid wearing western-type clothes?

Islam promotes modesty. It seeks to minimize vice and immorality in the society. A modest dress code is one way to achieve this social goal. Any garment which does not cover the "*awrah*" (part of the body that must not be revealed before any person) is forbidden in Islam. Awrah of a woman is all parts of her body except face and palm below wrist; and of a man from belly to knee.

Defining the purpose of garments, the Qur'an addresses the whole mankind in the following words:

"O children of Adam! We have bestowed raiment upon you to cover shame, as well as to be an adornment to you. But the raiment of righteousness, - that is the best." (7:26)

Thus the purpose of clothing according to the above divine text is elimination of shame and nudity and at the same time promote modesty and dignity in dress.

Ibn Umar reported that the Messenger of Allah said: "Whoever puts on a robe of fame in this world, Allah will dress him with a robe of disgrace on Resurrection Day."[15]

Style of men and women's garments is not a question to which Islam attaches any importance. When Islam moved into new areas and nations, ethnic people who adopted Islam continued to wear the types of dresses they used to wear before Islam with only amendment to eliminate sensuality and pride in dresses. No one suggested that they should wear what the Arabs used to wear. Muslims in Far East and South East Asia dress differently to Muslims in the Middle East. There are no restrictions in wearing European or Western dresses by Muslims so long they observe the modesty and dignity in their dresses. Many Muslim nations in Europe, Russia and China now use the dresses they used to have before Islam. Non-Arab Muslims wearing the Arabic dress do so in sheer love and respect of their Prophet and his companions which is highly commendable.

Any type of dress, which covers the *awrah* proper and does not look indecent, is permissible to wear. A dress that conveys an air of arrogance or pride of richness/position is discouraged in Islamic society.

39. What is Islamic Dress Code for Men?

Muslim scholars agree that a Muslim man must always cover the part of his body, which is described as *"awrah"*. And *"awrah"* of a man extends from the waistline down to the knees, both inclusive. According to some scholars a man's *awrah* is limited to his genitals and back passage.

Any type of dress, which covers the *awrah* proper and does not look indecent in behavior, is permissible to wear. A dress that conveys an air of arrogance or pride of richness/ position is discouraged in Islamic society.

40. What is the Dress Code For Women in Islam?

Quranic verse 31 of *Sura* 24, deals specifically with how women should appear in public and which groups of relatives are exempted from the general rule that governs women's dress.

"And say to the believing women that they should lower their gaze and guard their modesty, that they should not display their beauty and ornaments except what (ordinarily) appear thereof, that they should draw their veils over their bosoms and not display their beauty except to their......"(24:31)

The verse deals specifically with how women should appear in public and which groups of relatives are exempted from the general rule that governs women's dress. They may reveal their adornment in the presence of their husbands, fathers, fathers-in-law, sons, sons-in-law, brothers, nephews, other women, etc. The same verse includes the order that women "must draw their head covering which should be of ample length to be used to cover their bosom".

What is required of a Muslim woman is to have a dress that must not be eye-catching. A Muslim woman is required to maintain the normal Islamic standards of propriety. Whether she is attractive or not, the fact that she maintains these standards is sufficient to ensure that she is treated with respect and that people recognize that there is a virtuous woman and a woman of faith. What is forbidden to wear is any garment, which does not cover the "*awrah*", (the parts of the woman body that must not be revealed) before any person. According to jurists, the "*awrah*" of a woman is her whole body except her face and lower part of her hand and feet, Islam has not made any special requirements with regard to clothes, either for men or women. What is required is that the *awrah* must be covered, and that Muslim women should wear wide garments that are not eye-catching, too tight or transparent. The style of clothes is not a question to which Islam attaches any importance. When Islam moved into new areas, its ethnic people who adopted Islam continued to wear the types of clothes they used to wear before Islam. No one ever suggested that they should wear what the Arabs used to wear.

Hijab in Islam was legitimized in the revelation of the Quran in 33:59. The Qur'anic word in this verse used for outer-garment is *'jilbab'* and not *hijab*. Abdullah Yusuf Ali explains the word *'jilbab'* as "an outer garment; a long gown covering the whole body, or a cloak covering the neck and bosom."

"O Prophet! Tell your wives and daughters and the believing women that they should cast their outer garments over their persons (whenever they go out): that is most convenient, that they should be known (as such) and not molested. And Allah is Oft-Forgiving, Most Merciful."(33:59)

Thus a Muslim woman is required to wear dress that covers all her body, when she goes out of home or is in the company or presence of any man who is lawful to be married to her. She is not required to have her face or the lower part of her arms, i.e. from the wrist downward, covered when she goes out. Moreover she must not choose transparent or eye-catching material or colors for outer garments. These rulings apply to all Muslim women, married or unmarried, irrespective of clan and country.

There are numerous *Ahadith* (pl. of *Hadith*) both in favor and against using *Hijab* in public places. The prophet did not object in any instances. If a modest woman wants to wear a *hijab* (head cover) no one would stop her. But to say that it is obligatory for all women has no solid base.

Now let us come to our main issue of Muslim women living in the USA, Canada and Europe. Most of the Muslim women in these countries are either workingwomen or students in schools, colleges and universities, or housewives. It is obligatory for them to cover all parts of their body in loose dresses except their face and lower part of their arms while they go out of their home. A long loose shirt with a loose pant or knee-deep skirt with a scarf covering their head and bosom will suffice the requirements of the dress code for Muslim woman living in the West.

41. What kind of roles did women play in early & medieval Islam?

Women played important roles in the early Muslim community and in the very life of the Prophet. Muhammad's wife, Khadija bint Khuwailid was the first person to learn of the first Qur'anic revelations and she was the first believer. She owned her own business, hired Muhammad and later proposed to him. Historical pages are evidence that Arab women participated in battles, fought and nursed the wounded. They were consulted in important affairs of state and battles. Women of early Islam not only contributed to the collection and compilation of the Qur'an but also played an important role in the transmission of numerous *Ahadith* (pl. of *Hadith*; i.e. Prophetic traditions). They owned and sold property, engaged in trade and commerce and were encouraged to seek and provide educational instructions. Muhammad's wife Aisha and his daughter, Fatima played important roles in the Muslim community. How far women were independent in the community can be seen from the fact that many distinguished women converted to Islam before men in their family. Umar ibn al-Khattab, the second caliph, appointed women to serve as officials in the marketplaces of Medina. The Hanbali school of law supports the right of women to serve as judges. Ayesha bint AbuBak'r, the wife of the Prophet, personally conducted the insurrectionary movement against Ali, the fourth Caliph and commanded her own troops at the famous "Battle of Camel."

"In the early centuries of Islam, almost until the extinction of the Saracen Empire in the East, women continued to occupy as exalted a position as in modern society. Zubaida, the wife of Abbasid Caliph Harun, plays a conspicuous part in the history of the age, and by her virtues, as well as by her

accomplishments, leaves an honored name to posterity.......
Sukaina, or Sakina, the daughter of Husain and the grand-daughter of Ali, was the most brilliant, most accomplished, and most virtuous woman of her time........Buran, the wife of Caliph Mamun, Umm-ul-Fazl, Mamun's sister and Umm-ul-Habib, Mamun's daughter, were all famous for their scholarship. In the Fifth century of the Hijra, the Sheikha Shuhda, designated Fakhr un-Nisa (glory of the women) lectured publicly at the Cathedral Mosque of Baghdad to large audiences on literature, rhetoric, and poetry. Zat ul-Hemma, corrupted into Zemma, "the lion-heart", the heroine of many battles, fought side by side with the bravest knights.........
Comparatively the backward condition of Muslim Women in the present age is the result of a want of culture among the community generally, rather than of any special feature in the laws of fathers."[16]

42. What is *Shari'a*? How far it is applicable in the USA and Europe?

The *Shari'a* is derived from an Arabic root, meaning path or road. It is the path, which guides the Muslims to run their spiritual, moral, social, political and economic life in accord with Islamic principles. The purpose of this law is to design a system of rights and obligations, which would enable the community of believers to live a righteous life in this world and prepare them for the next.

Islamic law is based on submission to the Will of Allah. It is a way or path guiding the Muslims. Since Islamic law is based upon Islam, it covers all aspects of a Muslim life. The law governing all matters of life is known as ***Shari'ah***.

In essence, all of the *Shari'a* is contained in the Qur'an. It contains the principles of all the laws, further explained in the Sunnah of the Prophet, which constitutes the second source of Islamic law. This was further understood with the help of the consensus of the Muslim community, called *Ijma*. Finally, these three sources were complemented by human reasoning, called Qiyas, where necessary. Thus the *Shari'a*, the source of all laws of the Muslim community is revelation manifested through the Qur'an and explained through the Sunnah and then interpreted through *Ijma*, the agreed opinion of the jurists and finally *Qiyas* or human reasoning.

How far *Shari'a* is applicable in the life of the Muslims living today in Europe and America is one of the basic concerns here. This is not a new phenomenon for the Muslim society. Evidence of legal methodology dates back to the late seventh century. Schools of legal methodology came into being, each with its own peculiar emphasis on one or another aspect of juristic thinking. Variations in their thoughts and approaches occurred due to variations in the traditions and practices of the local neo-Muslims in various lands. Since each culture and ethnic group the Muslims met already had its own legal and religious history, the Muslims had to find ways to put their stamp on the conquered territory without destroying what they found there. They thus had to learn how to incorporate the "customary" law of the land, extending the umbrella of their own system. Our forefathers, when confronted with multi-racial and multi-cultural problems, interpreted the basics and fundamental Islamic teachings. Their interpretations satisfied the contemporary problems and people of their period. They faced the Greek philosophy, encountered the Babylonian, Egyptian, Persian, Indian and Roman civilizations and skillfully incorporated what was useful and in accord with *Shari'a* and discarded what was harmful and against the basic Islamic tenets.

The methodology of our forefathers can be the best guide for Muslims in Europe and America to shape their Western lifestyles in consonance with the basic Islamic tenets; to take what is good in the system and to dismiss what is bad for the community. At least we have the favorable environment here having freedom of religion, rule of law, and human rights, which are nonexistent in most of the Muslim countries of today. Numerous articles of American Constitution, especially the Bill of Rights and the Civil Liberty are in line with the principles of Islamic *Shari'a*.

43. What is *Sunnah* and what is *Hadith* (Tradition of the Prophet)? Are they synonym??

Originally, most Muslim scholars considered *Sunnah* virtually coextensive with *Hadith*: all that one could know, or needed to know, about the Prophet's example, one could find in the collected sayings. Gradually, the notion of Sunnah expanded to include not only the Prophet's reported words and anecdotes about his deeds, but the actual living practices of a certain community of believers.

The word *Sunnah* means literally a manner of acting, a rule of conduct, a mode of life. Practically it applies to sayings, conducts, and practices of the Prophet, his companions and later the conduct and practices of all the Muslim Ummah based on the divine instructions and *ahadees* of the Prophet.

Dr. Fazlur Rahman has summed up his views on the issue as follows:

> "The conclusions we have arrived at so far are first that the Sunnah and the Hadith were coeval and consubstantial in the earliest phase after Muhammad and that both were directed towards and drew their normativity from him…As the legal situations and the consciousness of moral and religious issues became more and more complex, controversies arose on most points, and in the theological and moral sphere especially there were foreign influences. But the concept of an ideal *Sunnah* was retained; whatever new material was thought out or assimilated, it was given as an interpretation of the principles of the Qur'an and the *Sunnah*."[17]

It may be gathered from the foregoing that the standard of conduct or the Sunnah of the Prophet set forth and introduced by the Prophet was not only valid and operative during his time for the Muslim community but it continued to remain so after him.

The Qur'an gives only a brief description of major issues and often deals with subjects in brief terms, leaving the details to be explained by the Prophet.

> "And We have sent down unto thee the Message;
> that thou mayest explain clearly to men what is sent
> for them."

In the Qur'an Muslims are commanded to pray and pay *Zakat.* It is thru Sunnah that the Muslims know the frequency and details of the Prayers and *Zakat* (alms). Most of the statements in the Qur'an needed further explanations before they could become guides for the Muslim community. The Prophet provided this explanation and clarifications, which were coded in his *Ahadees.*

The *Hadith* is a collection of the instructions, issued or the memoirs of the Prophet's conduct and behavior, as preserved by those who were present in his company or those to whom these were handed down by the first witnesses. These were later sifted and collected by divines and compiled in the form of books, among which the collections made by Malik, Bukhari, Muslim, Tirmizi, Abu Dawood, Nasa'i and Ibn Majah are considered to be the most authentic.

44. What are the Rules of Prohibition and Permissibility in Islam?

The fact that we regard everything as permissible in the first instance is based on what Allah states in the Qur'an that He has made everything on earth subservient to man. Allah has forbidden certain things only when they are harmful or evil to mankind. We have direct and explicit statement outlining what is forbidden to us. In Surah 6 Allah tells the Prophet to make this statement: "Say, come and I will make clear to you what Allah has forbidden you." This followed by a detailed list of serious sins and offenses, which relate to faith and social practices as well as the rights of others. In the same surah Allah tells us about the types of food He has forbidden us. The Prophet has told us that: "Everything that is harmful is forbidden." Another saying of the Prophet is "You shall not harm, nor reciprocate harm." The Qur'anic texts and the Prophetic statements are the best yardstick and guidelines to determine the permissibility or prohibition of every action of human life in respect of *ibadat* (matters relating to prayers) and *mu'amlat* (matters relating to human interactions).

The scholars of Islam are called upon to constantly evaluate whatever is introduced newly in our social life in order to give judgment on its permissibility or prohibition.

45. Why the Islamic Rules of Crime & Punishment so harsh?

The moral and logic behind the punishment for crimes in Islam is to establish security and safety of life, property and honor of individuals in the community as well as protection and stability of belief in God.

The punishment of theft in Islam is cutting off a thief's hand. "As to the thief, male or female, cut off his or her hands: a punishment by way of example, from Allah, for their crime: and Allah is exalted in power." (5:38).

Why theft or stealing is illegal in every civilized society? Any increase of money or material or any kind of benefits without earning it or buying it by a person is considered illegal in every community of society. The motive for stealing comes with the attempt to increase ones income or wealth without earning it. The fruits of his own labor do not satisfy him. Islam counters this motive by prescribing the punishment of cutting of thief's hand. Such a punishment will markedly decrease the thief's ability to work and reduce his income and wealth. The unmistakable result is that a thief will definitely end up in loss if he is punished with cutting off his hand, while he is more likely to profit if he receives a prison sentence. It is in human nature that people do not hesitate to do what is likely to bring them profit and to refrain from something, which makes loss a certainty. The Islamic punishment of theft is the most effective deterrent for a thief to keep him away from theft and stealing.

This punishment of cutting hand for theft is now-a-days limited to the theory of Islamic *shari'a* in most of the Islamic countries. Practically, it is non-existent in almost all the Muslim countries except Saudi Arabia and perhaps, in Sudan.

However, Allah has left the door open for those who repent and refrain from committing any crime in future, provided that he does not stop at this negative aspect but goes on to do what is positively good for the community. "But if the thief repent after his crime, and amend his conduct, Allah turns to him in forgiveness; for Allah is Oft-forgiving, Most Merciful."(5:39).

In case of adultery, the punishment of stoning to death is applicable only to a married adulterer/adulteress who has committed the offense. Anything less than that, such as element of doubt, does not incur that punishment. The Prophet tells us not to enforce a specified punishment once there is a doubt concerning the evidence, which seeks to prove the offence.

Islamic Law, called *Shari'a*, has some basic characteristics. The details of Islamic law cannot be implemented in isolation to the rest of the system in a society. We cannot simply take one legal provision and try to implement it in a social setup, which is not Islamic. Such an attempt is useless and such an action cannot be considered an implementation of Islam.

When the Muslim state of Medina was stricken by famine, Caliph Omar suspended the enforcement of punishment for theft. The servants of the son of Hatib ibn Abu Baltt'ah stole a camel, which belonged to a man of the tribe of Muzynah. When they were proven guilty, Omar ordered their hands to be cut off. However, on learning that their master kept them hungry, Omar stopped the enforcement of this punishment and punished their master, imposing a fine equivalent to the price of two camels. It is within this context that we should view the punishments imposed by Islam as a part of comprehensive system, which provides guarantees for all.

Every religions revealed by God comprise three essential aspects: a faith, a set of worship rituals, and a law to regulate human life. The people in authority and a mass of vested interests have always opposed the implementation of God's law. "It was We who revealed the Law (to Moses): therein was guidance and light.....do not sell My signs for a paltry price. If any do fail to judge by (the light of) what Allah has revealed, they are (no better than) unbelievers" (5:44). "We ordained herein (in Torah) for them: Life for life, eye for eye, nose for nose, ear for ear, tooth for tooth and wounds equal for equal. But if any one remits the retaliation by way of charity, it is an act of atonement for him. And if any fail to judge by (the light of) what Allah has revealed, they are (no better than) wrong-doers" (5:45).

These provisions outlined in the Torah have been retained in Islamic law as an integral part of it. The basic principle which is established through this concept is that of equality of human beings and equality before the law. This law acknowledges such an equality so as to make the punishment equal to the crime and to remove all considerations of class, position, lineage and race. All are equal before God's law since they all descend from one single soul created by God.

Retaliation on the basis of equality is the sort of punishment, which appeals to human nature. It quenches the desire for revenge, which may be fueled by blind fury, and it pacifies hearts and heals wounds.

Islam sees punishment as a deterrent. Its enforcement is not an objective. The Prophet advises his followers: "Anyone who commits something of this filth (adultery) should seek the cover of secrecy extended by God. If he comes to us with a confession, we must enforce punishment."

46. Who are Shiites and who are Sunnis?

These two terms apply to the two groups of Muslim community in the early period of Islam, which split on the question of succession of the Prophet of Islam, at the demise of the Prophet. Muslim Ummah chose Abu Bakr as the first caliph of the state. The followers of Ali ibn Abu-Talib, the cousin and also the son-in-law of the Prophet, considered him a legitimate candidate for the headship. The followers of Ali, Shian-e-Ali, became *'shittes'* while majority of the *ummah* was known as *'sunnis'*. The differences between the two arose on the question of political issue of headship of the *ummah*. Although Ali was chosen as the fourth caliph of the Islamic state, his followers considered him their First Imam (religious headship) and followed his progeny in succession of Imamate (religious headship).

Today Sunnis constitute approximately 85 percent and *Shias* make up 15 percent. The *shias* have significant numbers in Iran, Iraq, Bahrain and Lebanon and to some extent in India and Pakistan

Shia Islam developed three main divisions, stemming from disagreement over the number of Imams who succeeded Ali: the *Zaydis* recognized five Imams, the *Ismailis* recognized seven, and the Ithna Ashari (the twelvers) recognized twelve. The *Zaydis* split with others by recognizing Hussein's grandson Zayd as the fifth Imam. The *Zaydis* were the first Shia group to achieve independence. They founded a dynasty in Tabaristan on the Caspian Sea in 864 AD. Another Zaydi imamate state was founded in Yemen in 893 AD and lasted until 1963.

The split between the *Ismailis* (seveners) and *Ithna Ashari* (Twelvers) occurred in the eight century over the question of who succeeded the sixth Imam, Jafar al-Sadiq (d.765). The

Ismaili recognizes seven Imams, ending with Jafar al-Sadiq's son Ismail who predeceased his father and left no son. They formed a revolutionary movement against the Sunni caliphate of Abbasid dynasty and established the Fatimid Dynasty whose empire stretched from Egypt and North Africa to the Sind province of India between the tenth and twelfth centuries.

An Ismaili offshoot, the Nizari Ismailis, were particularly vehement in their violent opposition to Sunni Abbasid rule. Their tactics of violence and terror earned them the epithet of the Assassins. One of the Nizari leaders fled to India and established a line of Imams known by the honorific title of Agha Khan and created a nonviolent mainstream form of Shia that now has prosperous communities in Canada, Britain, East Africa and South Asia. The current Harvard-educated Agha Khan oversees the cultural and spiritual lives of his followers, in addition to looking after the educational, social and commercial institutions of the community.

The third and most populous Shia group, the Ithna Ashari (Twelvers), recognized twelve legitimate successors to Muhammad. The twelfth Imam, Muhammad al-Muntazar (the Awaited One) "disappeared" in 874 as a child with no sons, creating a major dilemma for the line of succession. Shia theology resolved this dilemma with the doctrine of the Hidden Imam, which declares that the twelfth Imam did not die but rather "disappeared" and is in hiding, or "osculation" for an unspecified period of time. This messianic figure is expected to return as the divinely guided Mahdi at the end of time to vindicate his followers, restore his faithful community, and usher in a perfect Islamic society of justice and truth. In the interim period, Shias are guided in religious matters by religious "mujtahid". In contrast to the majority Muslim experience, Twelver shias developed a clerical hierarchy at whose apex are religious leaders acknowledged by their followers as "ayatollahs" (signs of God) because of their knowledge and piety.

47. Can Muslims celebrate Christmas?

Some years ago I married an American girl who later converted to Islam. It so happens that my wife visits her parents with our children at every Christmas. The parents accept the fact that their daughter has become a Muslim and respect Islamic teachings with regard to food and drink when she is with them, to the extent that we do not see pork or an alcoholic drink on their dinner table during our visits. My wife gives them gifts at Christmas and they in return give her and my children presents at Christmas. I am sure our visit to my in-laws home and our social mixing with them are proper from Islamic point of view. Please advise.

A woman companion of the Prophet once told him that her mother had come to visit her, and that the mother was a non-believer who shared the pagan beliefs of the Arabs. She asked the Prophet whether it was appropriate for her to be kind and dutiful to her mother. The Prophet ordered her to be so.

You have been following the proper practice, which Islam urges by maintaining good relations with your wife's parents. There is no harm in giving them gifts on Christmas, because the Prophet did not instruct Muslims not to do so. On the contrary giving non-believers presents on their festive occasions is encouraged in Islam as long as they behave in proper manner and are not at war with Muslims.

48. Pl. specify the Islamic perspective in celebrating American holidays. Most of the Muslim kids celebrate American holidays along with their local counterparts of mixed faith.

One of the realities of being Muslim in the American context is having to decide whether or not to celebrate holidays that are part of the American—and often specifically Christian—calendar. Most of the Muslims see no reason not to observe the American holidays so long as it does not mean joining the celebrations with a lot of alcohol drinks and a lot of dancing and un-Islamic behavior.

A great many families observe American holidays that stress family relationships, such as Valentine's Day and particularly Mother's Day and Father's Day. In large part this reflects an interest in participating in customs that are particularly American. Muslims in America generally observes the two major national holidays, Memorial Day and Fourth of July, much as other Americans observe them, by attending fireworks or parades, having family picnics and relaxing.

Most of the Muslim parents and young adults and their children celebrate Halloween with other children in the neighborhood, dressing up in costumes and going door to door trick or treating. Thanksgiving with turkey at gatherings of family and friends is also one of the social occasions most Muslim families celebrate.

Of all the widely celebrated holidays in America, Christmas seems to provide the greatest dilemma for Muslim families. Although it is clearly a Christian holiday, it has become a national and social holiday as well. Even the religious aspect of the occasion is not irrelevant to Muslims who recognize Jesus Christ as a very important prophet whose birthday should be respected. Some families of mixed faith of Muslim men and Christian/Jews women or Muslim children and Christian or Jews mother celebrate Christmas with equal vigor and enthusiasm as other local Americans.

Islam does not forbid social contacts with people of other faith who are at peace and friendship with the Muslim community.

"Allah does not forbid you, with regard to those who do not fight you for (your) Faith nor drive you out of your homes, from dealing kindly and justly with them: for Allah loves those who are just."(8:60)

49. A Dialogue between Islam & Christianity

May I put to you certain viewpoints, presented by my friend, a Christian neighbor, which have had telling effects on us (my wife and me)? Perhaps you could enlighten us on these, putting before us the Islamic point of view.

I am taking the points raised by the author in his letter, one by one. Before I take up his points, I would like to remind him that to us Muslims, Jesus and Muhammad, peace be upon them both, are brothers in faith, as both of them were prophets chosen for the task of conveying God's message to mankind. As Muslims, we are required to believe in all of God's messengers and all prophets, making no distinction between them, and praising all of them for undertaking the task of guiding humanity along the right path. All the messages preached by all the prophets are essentially the same, based on the principle of the Oneness of God.

The first point mentioned by the writer is that "Jesus brought the dead to life, while the Prophet Muhammad executed people whom he considered to be wrongdoers."

Jesus Christ brought dead to life with God's will and permission. It was a miracle granted to him by God. Muhammad executed the wrongdoers by God's will and permission. Both the prophets followed the will and the order of God. Muhammad executed only those perpetrators of crimes for which God prescribed the death punishment. He was only carrying out God's orders and implementing His law. A murder is punishable by death in Judaism, Christianity and Islam. There is no evidence to suggest that the Prophet Jesus pardoned any murderer.

The second point concerns harboring wrong intentions and evil thoughts. The reader writes, "Jesus said, 'Even if you look at a woman with lust, your sin is as grave as adultery'. The Prophet Muhammad said that 'evil thoughts are not wrong and are permissible because God forgives them.'

Here the reader's attributing the statement of Muhammad needs some correction. The Prophet Muhammad never said that evil thoughts were not wrong, or they were permissible. What he said is that "God overlooks for my community what they contemplate until they put it in action." So long wrong intentions and evil thoughts are not put to practice nothing goes wrong and it is excusable. But if bad intentions are put to practice they are punishable. Prophet Muhammad is quoted to have said: "The eyes commit adultery through gazing, hands commit adultery through forceful action, and the legs commit adultery through walking and the mouths commit adultery through kissing."[18]

The third point is as follows: "At his dying moment, Jesus said, 'Father forgive them for they know not what they do'. The Prophet Muhammad cursed the Christians and the Jews on his deathbed."

No argument on the first part of the statement. What is attributed to the Prophet Muhammad in the second part of the statement is blatant lie. On his death bed Prophet Muhammad kept repeating these words, "Attend regularly to your prayers; be kind to your slaves and do not ask them to do what is beyond their ability. Fear God in your treatment of women." Moreover, at one point when he went to Taif to try to win acceptance of his message from its people, they ill-treated him, insulted him and instigated children and slaves to chase him out of the city. They even stoned and humiliated him and his feet were bleeding; his shoes full of blood. He took refuge in a garden, sat under a tree and addressed a heartfelt prayer to God. An angel came to him and said that he needed only his command and he was ready to bring the mountains over them. The Prophet said, "No I hope that God will bring them from among their offspring people who would worship Him alone."

The fourth point made by the reader is that "Jesus lived a sinless life, and did not marry, while Prophet Muhammad married several women and had sexual relationship with them."

What I find strange in my reader's point is that he implies that marriage is incompatible with piety from sin. But marriage is a legitimate practice that has been encouraged by God and by all the prophets of Old and New Testament, including Prophet Jesus. It is Christians who speak of marriage as "holy matrimony".

My reader's next point says, "Jesus forgave the sinful prostitute and asked the man without any sin to cast the first stone, meaning that everyone sins but are not caught red-handed like the prostitute. Prophet Muhammad condemned the sinful to death."

This is another example of how misinformed my reader is. Here Prophet Jesus reminded the people that all human beings are liable to commit sins, trivial and grave. Before any of them should think too well of himself, he should remember his own mistakes and sins. That is why he invited the person without a sin to cast the first stone. But this did not mean that the prostitute was forgiven. It was not open to the Prophet Jesus to waive God's punishment. It is again a false claim that the Prophet Muhammad condemned the sinful to death. If a punishable crime is committed and the perpetrator is identified in the proper legal manner that Islam prescribes, then the punishment must be enforced.

My reader then moves to the question of marriage and how Christianity emphasized monogamy and the permanency of marriage while Islam permits divorce and allows polygamy.

I think my reader does not know that polygamy used to be an acceptable practice among Christians until a couple of centuries ago. It is still practiced among the Christian tribes in Africa.

Polygamy flourished in a more or less pronounced form until forbidden by the laws of Justinian. But the prohibition contained in the civil law effected no change in the moral ideas of the people of Roman empire, Greece and Europe, and polygamy continued to be practiced until condemned by the opinion of modern society.

Both divorce and polygamy are allowed in Islam as solutions to insurmountable human and social problems.

The reader then moves to aspects of the second life saying that the Prophet Jesus explained that "the soul will be made into the image and likeness of God, and it will have continuous ecstasy engulfed in the love of God. Islam on the other hand speaks of giving each man sixty-nine wives with large almond-shaped eyes." He asks what does the soul have to do with wives in heaven? Will there be sexual pleasure for the soul?

This is another example where words are taken out of context and certain aspects are stressed while others, far more important, are overlooked. At no time does the Qur'an mention that any person will have so many wives in heaven. In deed, the term "wife" is not used at all in connection with the pleasures of heaven. The Qur'an speaks of the believers having companions in heaven. It is true that they are described as having very beautiful eyes and they are like "treasured pearls", but there is not even the slightest hint that there is any sexual relationship with those. All human generations will have had their chance and they receive their reward or punishment in the Hereafter.

My writer then refers to the creation of Jesus and that it is mentioned in both the Bible and the Qur'an that he was born to Virgin Mary who had conceived him through no physical contact with any man but with the Power of God. He asks, "Why did God choose a woman for the birth of Jesus, instead of bringing him into the world by some other means? Was Jesus right to claim that he was the Son of God?"

As for the first part of this question, which relates to the method of creation chosen by God, we Muslims have learned that God "cannot be questioned about what he does". We try to understand the wisdom and the purpose of anything that God may have chosen, but if we cannot find a satisfactory answer, we accept this as part of the work of God's free will. Had God chosen another method in the creation of Jesus, people would still ask why did He choose that one and not a different method.

As for the second part of this question, whether Jesus was right to claim that he was the Son of God. First of all, there is no evidence that Jesus made such a claim. The authenticity of this Gospel is a hotly debatable point. The earliest of the Gospels were written at least seventy years after God had raised him to heaven. "The Gospels of the New Testament were apparently written not by him nor by his closest followers in his own day, but decades later by more highly educated Christians who based their narratives on oral traditions that had been in circulation in the intervening years since his death."[19] It is not open to anyone to claim that he is the Son of God, because God simply does not beget children. The first creation of human being, Adam and Eve, did never claim to be the first son and first daughter of God.

My reader then moves on to the specific point of the Prophet's marriages with several women and says: "The Christians claim that the Prophet Muhammad had a weakness of the flesh (sex) and therefore married several widows under the pretext of looking after them."

His point is best answered by historical facts. The Prophet had his first marriage with Lady Khadeejah, a widow of 40 years of age, who was considerably older than him when he was only 25 and for 25 years he had no other wife and never contemplated marrying another woman. When Lady Khadeejah died, he was without a wife for sometime. All his later marriages came after he and his followers settled down in Madinah and established the Islamic State. Most of those marriages had special reasons; some were legislative, some political and others humanitarian. Polygamy was widely practiced in Arabia in those days and there was no limit of wives one could have. Islam limited this practice, allowing a man to have only four wives. The Qur'an says, "You may marry two, three, or four wives, but not more; if you cannot deal equitably and justly with all, you shall marry only one." If the claim you have mentioned was true, he would certainly have made no restriction on polygamy. Moreover, if he had the weakness of flesh, he would not have it dormant for more than 25 years when he was a young man of 25 years of age.

My reader's last point concerns that similarity between the Qur'an and the Old Testament. He claims that the Qur'an is an identical copy of the Old Testament. I have already explained that God's message is one. The Prophet Muhammad preached the same message of the Oneness of God, as did other prophets of Israel such as Abraham, Joseph, David, and Jesus. But it is certainly untrue to claim that the Qur'an is an identical copy of the Old Testament. My reader needs only take out the two books and read them.

50. Freedom of Belief

I do not believe that any of the great religions of the world now-a-days condone the use of force as a means of religious conversion. Could you please comment on whether the use of such conversion tactics today might be deemed acceptable?

The answer is 'No'. It is not acceptable to use force in order to compel people to hold any belief or religion other than their own. This applies today, in our modern civilized world, and it applies to all ages. Islam declares:

"Let there be no compulsion in religion..."(2:256)

With this clear order given in the Qur'an, we know the reason, why Islamic history has been distinguished for tolerance, freedom of belief, and absence of compulsion.

51. Is Islam tolerant to other religions?

Yes, historically and religiously Islam has a long record of tolerance to other religions. But now days some of the Muslim countries are intolerant to the "People of the Book" such as Taliban and al-Qaeda and sporadic conflicts between Muslims and Christians in Sudan, Nigeria, Pakistan, Iran and Indonesia.

The Qur'an clearly and strongly states that "Let there be no compulsion in religion...."(2:256) and that God has created not one but many nations and peoples. Many passages underscore the diversity of humankind. The Qur'an teaches that God deliberately created a world of diversity: "O mankind! We created you from a single (pair) of a male and a female, and made you into nations and tribes that you may know each other (not that you may despise each other). Verily the most honored of you in the sight of God is (he who is) the most righteous of you. And God has full knowledge and is well acquainted (with all things).(49:13).

The Qur'an and Islam recognize that followers of the three great Abrahamic religions share a common belief in the one God, in biblical prophets such as Moses and Jesus, in human accountability and in a Final Judgment followed by eternal reward or punishment. All followers of the three religions share the common hope and promise of eternal reward: "Surely, those who believe (in the Qur'an), and those who follow the Jewish (scriptures) and the Christians and the Sabians, and who believe in Allah and the Last Day, and work righteousness, shall have their reward with their Lord: on them shall be no fear, nor shall they grieve." (2:62).

Historically, while the early expansion and conquests spread Islamic rule, Muslims did not try to impose their religion on others or force them to convert. Jews and Christians were regarded as protected people (*dhimmi*) who were permitted to retain and practice their religions, be led by their own religious leaders, and be guided by their own religious laws and customs. For this protection, they paid a pool tax (*jizya*). While this amounted to second-class citizenship by our modern standards, it was very advance considering the age of seventh & eighth centuries. No such tolerance existed that time in Christendom, where Jews, Muslims, and other Christians (who did not accept the authority of the pope) were subjected to forced conversion, persecution or expulsion. In European history Inquisition knows the age.

In recent years, religious intolerance has become a major issue in self-styled Islamic countries like Iran, Sudan and Pakistan and in the hostile attitude of religious extremist organizations like Islamic Jihad (of Egypt), Jamat-e-Islami (Pakistan and Indonesia) and al-Qaeeda of Osama bin Laden, who are intolerant toward not only non-Muslim states but also Muslim states having good relations with Europe and America. Factually,the nature of most of the Muslim insurgencies against the West now a day are national and political. They are rooted in the post-colonial era when most of the Muslim countries were given self-rule to such authoritarian ruler who virtually was protector of the interests of the respective colonial power. The slogan of *jihad* is used by the insurgents to muster the public support of Muslim masses and to make it a fight of good-guy with bad-buy. This phenomenon is complex and has blinded the good senses of both the parties, making Muslims intolerant against the West and West, intolerant against the Muslims.

As far as I know, no society in the world, in the present age of history, is exclusively religious or exclusively non-religious. Even secular societies have religious flavor in their national life. It's a complex blending of moral and material wellbeing of mankind.

52. Can Muslims marry non-Muslims and Vice Versa?

Marriage regulations in Islam revolve around concerns regarding the faith of the children who will result from the union. Marriage between a Muslim man and someone from a community not possessing a revelation is considered unlawful. It is preferable for Muslim men to marry Muslim women. However, they are allowed to marry Christian or Jewish women, because they are "People of the Book", those who have divine revelations.

Muslim women must marry a Muslim or someone who converts to Islam. Under Islamic law, the male is recognized as the head of the household, and in marriage his wife is expected to take the nationality and status given by her husbands law. The man is also responsible for the religious instructions of his children and for serving as their guardian, particularly in matters of marriage. Thus the marriage of a Muslim woman to a non-Muslim man would result in the potential loss of the children's religion from this union. Hence it is not lawful.

However, the practices in the present age are different from theory. Interfaith marriages are there both in case of Muslim men and Muslim women not only in Europe and USA but also in India, Thailand, Australia, etc.

53. How do Muslims view Judaism and Christianity?

Judaism, Christianity and Islam are all monotheistic faiths and share a common belief in the oneness of God, His messengers and divine revelations, angels and Satan and in life hereafter. Muslims believe that God revealed His will through His prophets including Abraham, Moses, Jesus and Muhammad (Peace and blessings be upon them):

> "Say: We believe in Allah, and in what has been revealed to Abraham, Isma'il, Isaac, Jacob, and the Tribes, and in (the Books) given to Moses, Jesus, and the Prophets, from their Lord: we make no distinction between one and another among them, and to Allah do we bow our will (in Islam)."(Q.3:84)

The Qur'an regards Jews and Christians as children of Abraham and refer to them as "People of the Book". However, Muslims believe that Islam supersedes Judaism and Christianity and that the Qur'an is the final and complete word of God and that Muhammad (PUH) is the last of the prophets. Muslims believe that Moses and Jesus were given the Books from God, Almighty, and also believe what is written in the Old and New Testaments is a corrupted version of the original revelation to Moses and Jesus. Christianity's development of new dogmas such as the belief that Jesus is the Son of God and the doctrines of redemption and atonement are seen as admixing God's original revelation with human fabrication.

Muslims also believe in the virgin birth of Jesus. In fact, "Mary occupies a very important position in Muslim sacred history.... Sura 19 of the Qur'an is named after Mary and she is mentioned more often by name in the Muslim scripture than in the Christian scripture."[20]

All three faiths emphasize their special covenant with God, for Judaism through Moses, Christianity through Jesus, and Islam through Muhammad. Christianity accepts God's covenant with and revelation to the Jews but traditionally has seen itself as superseding Judaism with the coming of Jesus. Thus Christianity speaks of its new covenant and New Testament. So, too, Islam and Muslims recognize Judaism and Christianity: their biblical prophets (like Adam, Abraham, Moses and Jesus) and their revelations (the Torah and the Gospels). Muslim respect for all the biblical prophets saying "Peace and blessings be upon him" after naming any of the prophets. Muslims have common usage of names, like Ibrahim (Abraham), Musa (Moses), Da'oud (David), Sulayman (Soloman) and Issa (Jesus). In addition, Islam makes frequent reference to Jesus and to the Virgin Mary, who is cited more times in the Qur'an than in the New Testament. Popular Muslim lore ranks Virgin Mary among the "four most beautiful" women God created. The others were Asiya, martyred wife of the Pharaoh of Moses' time; Muhammad's first wife Khadija; and Fatima, the daughter of Muhammad and Khadija. The principal difference between Muslim and Christian views is that since Islam does not consider Jesus divine, Mary is not the mother of God, but mother of a prophet.

54. Friendship with non-Believers

Our present world is composed of multi-ethnic and multi-faith society. We Muslims have frequent dealings with non-Muslims and vice-versa, in our day-to-day life, especially in countries where the Muslims are in minority. What should be our line of behavior in the light of the following Qur'anic injunction?

"O you who believe! Take not for friends Unbelievers rather than Believers: do you wish to offer to offer Allah an open proof against yourselves?" (4:144)

This is the case of misleading translation of the Quranic verse. The term, 'waliy' in the Quranic verse has been rendered in translation as 'friend', which is inaccurate translation of the Arabic word, 'waliy'. The word, 'ally' is closer to the Arabic word, 'waliy'.

Some of the Quranic verses explain the purport and meaning of such kind of verses. A clear reference to this in the Qur'an is found in verses like 8 sura 60, which is as follow:

"Allah does not forbid you, with regard to those who do not fight you for (your) Faith nor drive you out of your homes, from dealing kindly and justly with them: for Allah loves those who are just."(8:60)

There are numerous texts of the Qur'an and the Traditions of the Prophet, which encourage Muslims to be kind to other religious communities. Thus on personal or public levels, there is nothing to stop any Muslim from forging a friendship with non-Muslims who harbor no ill intentions against Islam or its followers. The pages of Muslim history are full of such cordial relations with non-Muslims.

55. Greetings Exchanged on Ethnic Festivals

In most part of the world, multi-ethnic and multi-faith communities live side-by-side, like Jews, Christians, Muslims, Buddhists, Hindus and others. They congratulate each other at the time of festivals, like Christmas, Eid, Hanukah, Deevali, etc. How far a Muslim's participation is permissible at such an occasion?

It is clearly stated in the Qur'an that Allah likes us to be kind to those of the followers of other religions who do not try to fight us or turn us away from our land.

"Allah does not forbid you, with regard to those who do not fight you on account of your religion or drive you out of your homes, to treat them with goodness and to be just to them; truly Allah loves those who are just. "Indeed, Allah forbids you (only) with regard to those who fight you on account of religion and drive you out of your homes, and assist (others) in driving you out, that you turn to them (in friendship); and whoever turns to them (in friendship), they are wrongdoers." (60:8-9)

It is only those who are hostile to us and who try to turn us out of our land with whom we are not allowed having kindly relations. When different religious communities live peacefully together, it follows that they should congratulate each other on happy occasions. There is nothing wrong in that nor is it forbidden to partake of their food unless we know that the food offered is otherwise forbidden in Islam.

56. How did the early Muslim administrations deal with non-Muslim subjects? Did they allow freedom of religion??

Under the Umayyads, Muslim rule developed a policy begun under Omar (the second Caliph) that defined the socioreligious category of *dhimmi* (protected minority). Non-Muslims who chose not to convert enjoyed basic rights and freedom of worship so long as they paid a "poll tax" (*jizya*). The poll tax was a carry-over from both Roman and Sasanian practice. This poll tax was levied on non-Muslims in lieu of their military service. Muslims were required to pay the *zakat*, legally prescribed alms, which non-Muslims were not. *Kharaj*, the land tax, was levied to all land holdings, whether Muslim or non-Muslim. For legal purpose this *dhimmi* status meant that Jews and Christians were answerable to their own religions' jurisdictions rather than to Islamic religious law. Towards idolaters there was greater strictness in theory, but in practice the law was equally liberal.

In the reign of Othman, the third Caliph, the Christian Patriarch of Merv addressed the Bishop of Fars, named Simeon, in the following terms: "The Arabs who have been given by God the kingdom (of the earth) do not attack the Christian faith; on the contrary they help us in our religion; they respect our God and our Saints, and bestow gifts on our churches and monasteries."[21]

In order to avoid the least high-handedness, no Moslem was allowed to acquire the land of a *dhimmi* even by purchase. In the punishment of crimes there was no difference between the rulers and the ruled. If a Moslem kills a *dhimmi*, the former is liable to the same penalty as in the reverse case. The Caliphs of Baghdad (Abbasids), like their rivals of Cordova (Umayyads of Spain), created special departments for protection of the *dhimmis'* rights and interests. In the first century of Hegira we find important offices of state held by Christians, Jews and Magians. The Abbasid Caliphs, with some exceptions, recognized no distinction among their subjects of the score of religion. Under the Mogul Emperors of Delhi, Hindus commanded armies, administered provinces and sat in the councils of the sovereign.[22]

It must be added, however, that the bigoted views of the later Muslim canonists and the distinctive treatment of non-Muslims in some of the Muslim countries in the present age are based on political exigencies rather than religious bigotry.

57. How Mary and Jesus described in the Qur'an?

An entire surah 19 of the Qur'an is dedicated to Mary and her history. Mary is mentioned more times in the Qur'an than in the entire New Testament, and more biographical information about her is contained in the Qura'n than in the New Testament.

The Qura'nic account of Mary includes the pregnancy of her mother, Anna, Mary's birth, the annunciations of the coming births of John the Baptist and Jesus, and affirmation of the virgin conception and birth of Jesus: "And (remember) her who guarded her chastity: We breathed into her of Our Spirit, and We made her and her son a Sign for all peoples."(Q.21:91). The Quran also records Jesus as an infant verbally defending Mary's innocence in Sura 19, verses 27-34, in the following words:

> "At length she brought the (babe) to her people, carrying him (in her arms). They said: "O Mary! Truly an amazing thing you have brought! O sister of Aaron! Your father was not a man of evil nor your mother an unchaste woman!" But she pointed to the babe. They said: "How can we talk to one who is a child in the cradle?" He said, "I am indeed a servant of Allah: He has given me Revelation and made me a prophet; And He has made me blessed whosesoever I be, and has enjoined on me Prayer and Charity as long as I live; He has made me kind to my mother, and not overbearing or miserable; So Peace is on me the day I was born, the day that I die, and the day that I shall be raised up to life (again)!" Such (was) Jesus the son of Mary: (it is) a statement of truth, about which they (vainly) dispute."

Jesus is an important figure in the Quran. Like Christians, Muslims believe in the virgin conception of Jesus by God's Spirit. The Qur'an also records some of Jesus' miracles, including giving sight to the blind, healing lepers, raising the dead, and breathing life into clay birds (5:110).

Muslim and Christian beliefs about Jesus differ in two areas. First, Muslims do not believe that Jesus is the Son of God. They believe that he is one of the righteous prophets (6:83-87). Muslims believe that the Christian doctrine of Trinity is a form of polytheism, proclaiming belief in three gods rather than one God (4:171; 5:17; 5:72).

Second, Muslims do not believe in the crucifixion and resurrection of Jesus (4:157-58). They believe that although it appeared that Jesus was crucified, instead God took Jesus to Himself in a manner similar to what happened to Elijah (3:55; 4:157-58). Muslims do not believe in the Christian doctrine of Original Sin. Muslims believe that each of us will be held accountable before God for our own actions and thus responsible for our own salvation. No Moses, Jesus or Muhammad can save us from our sin.

58. How far the Islamic concept of 'Ummah' different from Nationalism?

At the outset of Muslim history, the concept of nationalism was based on the concept of Ummah. Muslims believe that they are members of a worldwide Muslim community, known as Ummah, united by a religious bond that transcends tribal, ethnic, place and national affiliation. This belief is based upon the Qur'anic text 2:143, which declares that "Thus have We made of you an Ummah justly balanced, that you might be witnesses over the nations....". Another verse: "The Believers are but a single brotherhood..."(48:10)

Islam appeared in a place and time in which tribal loyalty, called 'Asabiah' was considered the only identification. The individual's status was based upon his blood-ties or his affiliation with a particular clan or tribe. Islam declared absolute equality of all the believers in the new society. This notion of radical egalitarianism shattered the importance of tribal identities and fostered the belief that Muslims should always defend and protect other Muslims. "The believers, men and women, are protectors of one another. They enjoin what is just and forbid what is evil...."(Q.9:71).

This concept became particularly important during the nineteenth-century era of European colonialism and the rise of nationalism. Islamic resistance movements called for the defense of the *Ummah* against European intrusions throughout the Islamic world. The Ottoman Empire also appealed to the unity of the *Ummah* as a way of reviving Islamic solidarity. Muslim nationalist states although trying to unite their countries on the basis of national loyalty, did not challenge the authority of the concept of the *Ummah*. Contemporary Muslims still believe in the *Ummah* as a social identity despite the secularization of public life and contemporary emphasis on national political identities. Causes that have received broad attention and participation from the worldwide Muslim community include the Afghan struggle against Soviet occupation from 1979 to 1989, ethnic cleansing of Bosnian Muslims in 1994 and Kosovo Albanian Muslims in 1997, and the ongoing struggle of the Palestinians. Muslim Ummah has also been active in fund-raising to assist victims of natural disasters in the Muslim world, such as earthquakes in Turkey, Afghanistan and Pakistan.

59. What is the Islamic concept of 'Jihad'? Does it promote terrorism?

In Arabic, 'Jihad' literally means to strive, to exert oneself to the utmost of one's capacity. A person who exerts himself/herself physically or mentally or spends his/her wealth in the way of Allah is indeed engaged in Jihad. Jihad can in fact consist of speaking the truth before a despotic ruler, applying oneself in the pursuit of knowledge, or even struggling internally against one's own weaknesses and vanity. According to one tradition, the Prophet tells his followers, on return from battle, that they have now returned from the 'lesser Jihad' (battle) and must turn to the 'greater jihad' (the inner struggle for true submission to God). In short Jihad means struggle for a just cause. However, in the language of *Shari'a*, this word has been used inter-alias for the war waged solely in the name of Allah for Allah and against those who perpetrate oppression as enemies of Islam. This supreme sacrifice of lives devolves on all Muslims. If, however, a section of the Muslims participate in the Jihad, the whole community is absolved of its responsibility. But if none comes forward, everybody is guilty. This concession vanishes for the citizens of an Islamic State (a truly Islamic State) when it is attacked by an enemy power. In that case everybody must come forward for the Jihad. In all these cases, Jihad is as much a primary duty of the Muslims as are the daily prayers or fasting.

The Islamic concept of Jihad as war, battles and skirmishes was devised in the historical background of the Muslim community at the outset of its history. The community, in the beginning, faced oppression and enmity of Arabian tribes of Makkah. Enemies of Muslims and Islam were determined to oust Muhammad and his community from Makkah, going to the extent to kill him. Fighting was allowed to the oppressed community in self-defense for survival.

"Fight in the cause of Allah
Those who fight you
But do not transgress limits;
For Allah loveth not transgressors." (2:190)

Explaining the meaning of this verse, most of the Qur'an commentators agree on the following explanation: "War is permissible in self-defense, and under well-defined limits. When undertaken, it must be pushed with vigor, but not relentlessly, only to restore peace and freedom for the worship of Allah. In any case strict limits must not be transgressed: women, children, old and infirm men should not be molested, nor trees and crops cut down, nor peace withheld when the enemy comes to terms."

Though the defense of Islam by means of *Jihad* is not a fundamental tenet, but its need and importance have been repeatedly emphasized in the Qur'an and the Sunnah (Traditions of the Prophet). It is in essence a test of sincerity and faithfulness of believers in Islam.

There are numerous verses in the Qur'an and numerous *ahadith* (pl.of *Hadith*) on the subject. Their justifications of jihad cannot be seen in isolation. They are all contextual. They can be seen only in conjunction with the perpetual hostility of the forces inside and outside of Arabia. The tactics of offence, at times, was the only way to maintain the survival of the nascent *ummah* who was beset by the might and power of Byzantium and Persia.

According to the discourses of the medieval jurists and thinkers on the subject, three forms of jihad emerged in Islamic History. The original form of jihad was a perpetual state of war waged against non-Muslims in order to convert the world to Islam. According to this theory the world is divided into two perpetually hostile spheres: the abode if Islam (*dar al-Islam*) and the abode of war (*dar al-harb*). The abode of Islam is under an obligation to conquer the abode of war. The second form was defensive in nature. It emerged during the period of Crusades when Muslims attempted to regain lost territories. The third form *ghaza* model, was an offensive jihad during the Ottoman period. Pursuant to the *ghaza* model, Muslims were obligated to wage war to enlarge the territory of Islam. However, the division of the world into an abode of Islam and an abode of war was functional, not theological. The idea of a unified abode of Islam existing in a state of mutual hostility with the rest of the world was the product of a specific historical context that generated a normative ideal. This ideal was always under serious challenge because the abode of Islam was rarely united and furthermore it was difficult to maintain a perpetual state of hostility between Islam and its neighbors. In response to this challenge, jurists from the Shafi'i school of thought introduced the notion of abode of treaty, reconciliation or peace. Such an abode consisted of territory that had a treaty or agreement with the abode of Islam; therefore Muslims were under no obligation to conquer it.

The juristic theory of jihad has always been changing and redefining in the changing circumstance of history. The jurists' position was thoroughly contextual and historical, not necessarily moral or theological. Contemporary Islam has had no problem adopting the idea of defensive *jihad*. Even Muslim fundamentalists insist that they are fighting either to defend the integrity of their state against despotic rule inherited from their colonial power or to regain occupied territory. On no occasion in recent memory have Muslims pursued a *jihad* in order to convert the world.

As regards the other part of the question as to "how far the concept of jihad promotes terrorism" let's first ask what is terrorism?

To date, the international community has been unable to reach a universally accepted definition of "terrorism". For sake of convenience, we can use the following as a working definition of terrorism: "any violent acts or the threat of violence against third parties, often innocent civilians, to achieve political concessions or changes in policies by states or persons in authority".

Historically, sympathy for perpetrators of terrorist acts confronting a more powerful foe while engaged in a struggle on behalf of peoples denied rights and freedoms is not strange. Such attitudes inevitably affect judgments about which acts may be characterized as terrorism. One party's terrorist might be another's freedom fighter. Thus it would be rare to find any group or government, Muslim or non-Muslim that is involved in acts that would fit in the above definitions of terrorism.

Despite the inability of the international community to agree concerning what falls with the category of "terrorism", there is agreement that acts of international terrorism contravene international law. Thus there are international conventions designed to promote international cooperation in preventing and punishing terrorism.

Mainstream Islam does not condone terrorism, whether intrastate or international. The connections between Islamic institutions and doctrines and any form of terrorism are very weak. Islamic rules of engagements are well defined as in the earlier explanation of the Qur'anic text. Of course, there are Muslims who sponsor or perpetrate terroristic acts either in a governmental or private capacity. While Muslims who engage in acts of what others would characterize as terrorism may have subjective convictions that their acts are undertaken pursuant to the dictates of their religion, these beliefs have very tenuous foundations in Islamic law or theology. General perception should not obscure the fact that Muslim terrorists use the same tactics and pursue basically the same kinds of political agenda as do non-Muslim organizations involved in terrorism, such as Irish Republican Army, the Jewish Defense League, Basque separatists, Tamils in Sri Lanka, Sikh separatists, the Japanese Red Army and other groups involved in terrorist activities. Any balanced survey of the record of international terrorism would establish that there is no uniquely Islamic proclivity to condone or indulge in acts of international terrorism.

Nonetheless, Islam has become closely associated with terrorism in the minds of people in the West, especially after 9/11 attack on New York World Tower. The Western media have propagated the notion that there exists a natural connection between terrorism and Islamic fanaticism and militancy. While Western media and intelligencia link the recent terrorist violence in London, Spain, and other places with Islamic phenomenon, political analysts view the roots of terrorism lay in political autocracy and foreign occupation of the territory.

The issue of colonialism is one that most westerners rarely think about or ignore it, but which is of great concern to many in the Middle East, North Africa, and South Asia, especially to the Muslims living in these regions. Throughout the Middle East and North Africa, once occupied by the British and the French, were primarily Muslim. The native populations of these regions were rarely treated well. Many Palestinians, for example, are convinced that the current unrest in their region exists because the British, French and the United Nations cheated them out of land that had been theirs for centuries. Many Muslims still feel that American involvement in the

Persian Gulf represent nothing more than the old colonialism in new clothes. Colonialism is a sore issue with Muslims all over the world. When we try to understand the motivations behind alleged Islamic calls for *jihad* all of these issues must be kept in mind.

60. What is Fundamentalism? What does Islamic Fundamentalism mean?

Reassertion of religion in politics and society has been summed up by the press and publications and by the intellects and academics under the term 'Fundamentalism'. All those who call for a return to foundational beliefs or the fundamentals of religion may be called fundamentalists. Thus the term Islamic fundamentalist could include all practicing Muslims, who accept the Qur'an as the word of God and the Sunnah of the Prophet as a model for living.

The understanding and perceptions of the term, 'fundamentalism' are heavily influenced by American Protestantism and European Catholicism emphasizing the literally interpreted Bible as fundamental to Christian life and teachings in 20th century. For many liberals or mainline Christians, fundamentalist is derogatory, being applied to all those who advocate a literalist biblical position and thus are regarded as retrogressive and extremist. As a result, fundamentalism often has been regarded popularly as referring to those who are literalists and wish to return to and replicate the past.

Fundamentalism is often equated with political activism, extremism, fanaticism and terrorism. This term has been applied to the governments of Libya, Saudi Arabia, Pakistan, Iran and Sudan. The only phenomenon common to these states is the fact that their rulers have appealed to Islam to legitimize their rule or policies. Otherwise Libya was not as Islamic as it was on the path of socialism, Saudi Arabia used religion to legitimize a conservative monarchy; Zia ul-Haq's Nizam-e-Islam in Pakistan was more liberal and friendly to the west and United States. Iran under the Ayatollah Khomeini was highly critical, even condemnatory of the West, often at odds with the international community and regarded as a radical terrorist state.

To me the term, Islamic Fundamentalism, is too laden with Christian perceptions and Western stereotypes, implying a monolithic threat. I think more fitting term is "Islamic revivalism" or "Islamic Resurgence". Islam possesses a long tradition of revival (tajdid) and reform (islah), which includes notions of political and social activism dating from the early Islamic centuries to the present day.

"The Western media often give the impression that the violent form of religiosity known as "fundamentalism" is a purely Islamic phenomenon. This is not so. Fundamentalism is a global fact and has surfaced in every major faith in response to the problems of our modernity. There is fundamentalist Judaism, fundamentalist Christianity, fundamentalist Hinduism, fundamentalist Buddhism, fundamentalist Sikhism, and even fundamentalist Confucianism."[23]

Of the three monotheistic religions, Islam was in fact the last to develop a fundamentalist strain, when modern culture began to take root in the Muslim world in the late 1960s and 1970s. By this date, fundamentalism was quite well established among Christians and Jews, who had had a longer exposure to the modern experience.

61. What are the Islamic Views on Human Rights and Social Justice?

Islam, at its outset, established that no human is infallible and no ruler is immune to accountability. Two early documents form the basic charter of human rights. The first, known as the "Constitution of Medina". It has set out the principal terms governing the relationships of Muslims to one another and to the non-Muslim groups in the region equating them both as equal citizen of the State of Medina.

"This document, which has been carefully preserved in the pages of Ibn-Hisham, reveals the Man in his real greatness—a master-mind, not only of his own age, but of all ages....he set himself to the task of reconstructing a State, a commonwealth, a society upon the basis of universal humanity."[24]

The other is the "Farewell Sermon" which the Prophet of Islam, at the occasion of his last pilgrimage, declared to the multitude of people: "You all descend from Adam and Adam was created out of clay. No Arab is superior to a non-Arab and no white has any privilege over a black, except through good deeds based on fearing Allah. The best among you are those who are most God-fearing. Your lives and property are sacred and inviolable among one another. Nothing that belongs to another is lawful to his brother, unless freely given. Guard yourself against committing injustice."

In principle, the equality of all human beings has always been central to the Islamic social concept. Muslim history is full of examples of "the triumph of the universalistic spirit", in which Muslims and non-Muslims lived together in harmony. At times, however, especially in the present age, the spirit of "partisanship" has dominated, with disastrous consequences. In the beginning, this equality is clearly reflected in the treatment of slaves and non-Muslim populace as regulated in the Islamic system. Islam could not abolish slavery at one strike. This was a worldwide system operated by all countries and nations. Islam laid down a system, which ensured the gradual and steady eradication of the system of slavery and its progressive abolition.

A "Universal Islamic Declaration of Human Rights," promulgated in 1981 by Islamic Council, a nonauthoritative body made up of invited members from a number of Middle Eastern and south Asian Muslim countries, represents one of the fullest recent articulations of Islamic values on the subject. The document affirms a "commitment to uphold the following inviolable and inalienable human rights that we consider are enjoined by Islam"—right to life, freedom, equality, justice, fair trial, protection against abuse of power, torture, protection of reputation, asylum, minority protection, participation in public affairs, freedom of belief, freedom of thought and speech, freedom of religion, free association, economic order, protection of property, worker dignity, social security, family integrity, protection of rights of married women, education, privacy, freedom of movement, and freedom of residence. In 1990 the Organization of the Islamic Conference, whose membership includes representatives of virtually all the nations with majority Muslim populations, put forth a 'charter of rights', though it differs from the International Bill of Human Rights of the United Nations in that the Islamic charter continues to subsume all rights under the controlling authority of religious law, or *shari'a*.

In its ideals, Islam has always been a highly service-oriented tradition with a keen sense of social responsibility. Among the earliest and most insistent themes in the Qur'an is the call to establish economic justice and to attend to the needs of society's marginalized and disadvantaged. Life in seventh-century Mecca was especially hard for orphans and widows, as well as for the poor. Observing the alarming gap between the haves and have-nots, the Prophet issued a challenging response in the form of Qur'anic texts and gave further views on matters of social justice in his Hadith (traditions).

"Do you see one who denies the Judgment (to come)? Then such is the man who repulses the orphan (with harshness), And does not encourage the feeding of the indigent, So woe to the worshippers who are neglectful of their prayers; those who (want but) to be seen (of men), but refuse to give even neighborly needs"(107:1-7).

Numerous other texts call on Muslims to freeing a slave, feeding an orphan, exhort one another to perseverance and encourage each other to compassion.

Countless *ahadith* likewise speak of the need for social awareness and action.

62. Co-Education: What is the Islamic view on co-education?

There is a well-known principle in Islamic law, which may be rendered in translation as *"prevention of means"*. This applies to any situation or condition, which may be permissible in the first instance, but is calculated to lead to something harmful for the society and hence, forbidden. Co-education is one such case. In the first instance, there is no harm in a group of people, men and women, or boys and girls, to be present in a classroom where a teacher is giving a lesson. But when we put together a group of young boys and girls, close to the age of adolescence, in the relaxed environment of a school where they meet and play, then it is asking too much of such young people to observe Islamic standards of morality. The result may be very serious indeed. Therefore, we can say that coeducation is unacceptable in an Islamic society, because of what it leads to, not because of the process of teaching or of the meeting of the two sexes in a classroom. There is no harm in co-education of boys and girls up to a certain age.

The ever-increasing number of teenage pregnancy in countries where co-education is permissible is a clear proof of its social implications.

63. Dancing: Is dancing permissible in Islam?

There is no specific ruling concerning dancing, just like many other activities. Decent dancing which does not aim at arousing sensual emotions, and does not make of the women's body an object of exciting desires, is permissible. Folk dancing is acceptable from the Islamic point of view.

When a delegation from Abyssinia visited the Prophet, they performed some of their folk dancing in the mosque. The Prophet watched them and he also let his wife, Aisha, watch the show.

64. Statues & Sculptures: What is wrong in commemorating great heroes of Islam by erecting their statues or displaying their figure-photos in prominent places?

Islam discourages excessive glorification of people, how great they may be, whether they are living or dead. The Prophet (pbuh) is reported to have said, "Do not glorify me in the same manner as the Christians glorify Jesus, son of Mary, buy say, 'He is a slave of Allah and His Messenger.'"[25]

He forbade his companions, who used to stand up to greet him out of respect saying, "Do not stand up as the Persians do, some people honoring the others." [26]

He warned his followers against praising him excessively after his death, saying: "Do not make of my grave a site for festivals." And he prayed to his Lord, "O my Lord, do not let my grave be made into an idol to be worshiped."[27]

The Messenger of Allah (pbuh), the caliphs, the monarchs, and the great Imams of Islam were never immortalized in figures or statues. In Islam the fathers tell their children, and they pass on to their own children, the stories of their heroes' deeds and achievements. At meetings, gatherings, and celebrations, these stories are told and retold, filling the hearts and minds of Muslims without any need for their pictures and statues.

65. Decorative Figurines

I collect rabbit and cat figurines as a hobby. Some of these are more stylized and abstract while others are more realistic. Some people object to them. They are not more than charming decorations. What is the proper view of Islam on visual arts?

Islam, like Judaism shares the deep-seated concern over graven images and has never developed a tradition of religious sculpture. Muslim artists have refined a number of spectacular two-dimensional expressions of religious themes and images. Calligraphy, illumination, and illustration are the three most important.

Decorative figurines are not statues. They are not thought of idols by anyone. There is no harm in using such things for home decorations.

66. Is Mercy Killing permissible in Islam?

Killing is permissible in Islam only as punishment for death penalty of certain well-proved crimes OR in case of justified battle. All other killings are forbidden in Islam. Even if a person wishes to die, and even if his wish is the result of suffering a long, incurable illness, terminating his life is forbidden. To put a person on 'mercy killing' is an assault on nature's authority.

Whoever takes his life by any means whatsoever has unjustly taken a life, which God has made sacred. Life is a trust given to man by God. He is not allowed to diminish it, let alone to harm or destroy it. Allah says: "Do not kill yourself; indeed, Allah is merciful to you." (4:29). The Prophet warned that anyone who commits suicide will be deprived of the mercy of Allah and will not enter the Paradise. The Prophet said:

"In the time before you, a man was wounded. His wounds troubled him so much that he took a knife and cut his wrist and bled himself to death. Thereupon Allah said, 'My slave hurried in the matter of his life.' Therefore, he is deprived of the Garden."[28]

67. Can Muslims migrate to non-Muslim countries and live there for good?

Emigration of Muslims to non-Muslim countries for economic, political, sectarian, religious and like persecutions in their host countries is permissible for certain period of time; but whether to live for good in a non-Muslim country, Islamic scholars and jurists are divided in their opinion. "The general consensus of the classical jurists is, no. It is not possible for a Muslim to live a good Muslim life in an infidel land. He must leave home and go to some Muslim country. If a Muslim land is conquered by the Christians, like Spain, may they stay under Christian rule? The answer of many jurists was again no, they may not stay. The Moroccan scholar, al-Wansharisi, considering the case of Spain, asks if the Christian government is tolerant and allows them to practice their religion, may they then stay? His answer was that in that case it is all the more important for them to leave, because under a tolerant government, the danger of apostasy is greater."[29]

When atrocities and persecutions of Meccan Qureish became intolerable for the new-Muslim community, the Prophet allowed a group of Muslims to migrate to a Christian country, Abyssinia. The only basic problem for a Muslim in a non-Muslim country now a day is how to live a good Muslim life. Whether it is a wise and correct decision for a Muslim to migrate Europe and America is a highly personal and individual question. Everyone can judge his own circumstances best. But no person, while taking such a decision, should ignore the pros and cons, especially with regard to what may happen to his children's identity and their future.

"If you are confident that you can live here in conformity with the will of God, and you are being useful to Islam, and are safeguarding your own faith as well as caring for the faith of others, and are also engaged in economic activities according to your needs, then it is all right, and I will even say that your stay is propitious."[30]

68. Is Smoking permissible in Islam?

Muslim scholars are very hesitant when they come to the issue of smoking, whether permissible or prohibited. Historically, we hardly find the customary habit of smoking in the people of Arabia during the time of advent of Islam, although now it is customary in almost all Middle Eastern countries to smoke '*habli-babli*', a traditional smoking. Hence there is no mention in the Qur'an and no Hadith on smoking. The Qur'anic text listing the forbidden things does not include smoking. However, there are certain principles of Islamic legislation that can apply in all such cases where the Qur'an and the Hadith are silent. The Hadith that "there shall be no infliction of harm on oneself or others" is good for analogy in the case of smoking. The recent medical findings in Europe and America have concluded that cigarettes and drug smoking are harmful for the health of the smokers. Smoking in all the public places and offices and ads for cigarettes in all kinds of media have been banned in many countries of Europe and Americas. On the analogy of the above fact it can be easily determined whether smoking is permissible or prohibited in Islam.

69. What does Islam say about homosexuality?

Like Christians and Jews, Muslims consider sexual fulfillment within marriage for husband and wife to be the ideal state of affairs in society.

"Your wives are a tilth unto you; so approach your tilth when or how you will..." (2:223)

Sex in marriage is considered a means of communication and pleasure and is not restricted to procreation. In Islam homosexuality is a crime punishable under Islamic law. Some Islamic countries adhere to it and some tolerate it. The jurists have held different opinions concerning the punishment for this practice. Should it be same as the punishment for fornication, or should both the active and passive participants be put to death?

Homosexuality is perversion of sex and a reversal of the natural order, a corruption of man's sexuality and a crime against the rights of females.[31] The story of the people of Prophet Lut (Lot) as narrated in the Qur'an should be sufficient for us.

70. Boy Meets Girl and Dating

I could not find any ruling in the Qur'an or the Hadith forbidding a man going out with a woman. It is quite natural to be attracted to the opposite sex. It seems to me that such a meeting, or going out, is permissible. If you disagree, how could you justify your ruling, when it is Allah who has made this mutual attraction a part of our nature?

It is true that Allah has placed this sex pull in our nature. Otherwise, humankind would not have been preserved. Allah, however, wants us to satisfy our natural desire in a clean, legitimate way. Therefore, He regulated the relationship between the two sexes on the basis of marriage.

This applies to every natural desire common to all mankind. We need to eat in order to live and there is a natural desire to eat which is common to all people. Unlike animals, which satisfy their hunger in a mechanical, instinctive way, man has refined his approach to food and clothing so as to make them part of human civilization. All agree that only things obtained in a legitimate manner are permissible to eat. We cannot just take what does not belong to us. We have to buy it or be given it as a gift. Otherwise, we commit a sin and a felony if we take it away. The same applies to the satisfaction of natural tendencies of establishing a relationship with must be legitimate and the only legitimate relationship in this connection is that of marriage. The fact that the attraction is natural does not mean that we can seek its satisfaction in an unruly or undisciplined manner. Its satisfaction is regulated within the marriage institution. This distinguishes Islamic society by its clean, healthy relationship.

It is forbidden in Islam for a man to be alone with a woman who is not his wife, or a very close relative, in a room where they cannot be seen. This is not due to any lack of trust in either the man or the woman. It is only meant to strengthen them against any temptation. Abdullah ibn Abbas quotes the Prophet as saying: "Let no one of you be alone with a woman except in the presence of a relative whom she may not marry." (Al-Bukhari and Muslim). Ahmed ibn Hanbal also relates a hadith in which the Prophet is quoted to have said: "He who believes in Allah and the Last Day must not be alone with a woman without the presence of a close relative of hers which she may not marry. Otherwise Satan would be the third one with them." There is no objection in having a company of opposite sex in a marketplace or classroom.

71. Video and Photography

Video and photography were not invented in the time of the Prophet. Hence there is no reference in the Qur'an and *Ahadees* on this subject. We find references in *Ahadees* on making sculpture, statues, shapes and engraving on stone or wood. In a Qudsi Hadith, the Prophet quotes Allah as saying: "Who does a greater sin than one who tries to create something like My creation. Let them create a particle or a seed or a barley seed."[32] Muslim scholars are unanimous that making of sculptures, statues, shapes and engravings on stone or wood to create likeness of Allah's creation is forbidden in Islam.

Sheikh Mohammad Bakheet, a former Mufti of Egypt has made it clear that photography or video is not included in such prohibition. This is no more than an art of capturing a reflection by special technique. Using a camera to take a picture is similar to fixing what we see in a mirror. The lens in a camera only captures a mirror picture of the person or object for which we need a photo. The same theory applies to video camera. It does no more than taking a large number of still pictures which when shown in rapid succession, create the image of movement.

72. How can a Muslim practice obligatory rituals of Islam in a life-style of Europe, Canada & America?

From the very beginning of the Islamic era, Muslims have been living in non-Muslim countries of different denominations. Early conquest and expansion of Islamic state made the believers of Makka and Medina settle in Egypt, Syria, Iraq and Iran, then all non-Muslim countries. Within a century, the Arab Muslims spread over from Morocco to Sind in the Indian subcontinent. Muslims living in those countries adapted themselves with the living conditions of the local populace without violating the basics of Islam.

Early Muslims, unlike contemporary Muslims, knew well that the religion of Islam is good for all lands and all nations. It is universal, not territorial. "A guidance to all mankind and clear proof of the Guidance and the Criterion" (Q.2:185).

There is one difference of course. Classical Muslims were rulers and had full control and freedom to shape their lifestyle in line with their religious traditions while they allowed religious freedom to non-Muslims to shape their life according to their social and religious customs. Contemporary Muslims living in non-Muslim countries now-a-days do not have this prerogative. Muslims living in minority in non-Muslim countries like Europe, Canada and America, though enjoy religious freedom, they face cultural problems, sometime at conflict with the tenets of Islam. Matters relating to faith and worship (prayers, fasting, almsgiving, and pilgrimage) are no problem. But matters relating to social interactions, culture and traditions, raising family and children on Islamic way of life are basic problems. All the countries abovementioned are secular, non-religious and pluralistic in social composition. There are Buddhist and Hindu temples, Jews synagogues, Muslim mosques in addition to Christian churches of

Catholics and Protestants in almost all the above countries. All have freedom to go to their temples and pray according to their religions. Islam is a bit different from the 'People of the Book' or people of other faith. It asks its followers not only to have full faith in the Oneness of God and the Book of Qur'an, the Word of God, revealed through His Messenger, Muhammad (PUH). It also demands from its followers to lead their all aspects of life according to the principles set by the Quran and Sunnah of the Prophet.

Shari'a, the Islamic Law, is basically based upon the verses of the Qur'an and sayings and practices of the Prophet. Companions of the Prophet, and their later two generations, knew well the spirit of Islam. They knew to use *Shari'a* in different circumstances. They introduced changes in *Shari'a* relating to the social and administrative legislation of the community. Specially, the Second caliph, Umar introduced certain changes set by the Quran and Sunnah, saying that the situation had changed since the time of the Prophet. There are many examples of this kind. The scope of this paper does not permit me to put all such instances here. The gist of the discussion here is that the *Shari'a* Law changes with the change of time and change of place and even change of circumstances in one place and in one time. The caliphs of Umayyad and Abbasids and their satellite rulers in different parts of their kingdom used this latitude of Islamic jurisprudence to their full benefits and interpreted *Shari'a* to fit their interests.

Muslims now living in a secular and pluralistic society are not obligated to follow all the rulings of *Shari'a* followed in a Muslim dominated country. It was not the mission of Islam to build up a structure of conduct and action that was rigidly fixed for all time irrespective of the change of time and circumstances. The Prophet gave to his followers the lines of guidance, which enabled them to build a fresh structure of action and conduct under changed circumstances. This kind of flexibility can be seen in the behavior of the Prophet's Companions. They did one thing in Egypt, another in Syria and still another in Iraq. For we Muslims, now living in America, Europe and Canada, I put below the following guidelines that will help us lead to a successful life living with Islamic legacy.

First, all those living in the USA, Canada and Europe, identifying themselves as Muslim, need to have a basic knowledge of Islam by getting help from the original source of the Qur'an and the Sunnah of the Prophet and his companions. This will help them and their posterity.

Second, we must try to observe the daily obligatory prayers, fasting in the month of Ramadan, distribution of *Zakat* (almsgiving) and charity, once a year and pilgrimage of Makka, once in lifetime. We must try to observe these pillars of Islam as much as possible in our living circumstances so long we live as Muslim in non-Muslim secular countries. Only five times prayers are daily obligation; fasting and *Zakat*, once a year and Hajj, once in lifetime. One may find difficult to observe all or some of the above tenets of Islam, like five times daily prayers, in the style of life we are in here. Allah says, "And strive in His cause as you ought to strive. He has chosen you, and has imposed no difficulties on you in religion...." (Q.22:78). Know that one becomes Muslim only by pronouncing the simple 'Shahada' (testimony), "There is No deity, but God and Mohammad is his Messenger." A Muslim remains Muslim even if he doesn't observe any or all the above tenets of Islam, *not by choice*, but by necessity of circumstance. But being Muslim is a great responsibility. "You are the best of peoples, evolved for mankind, enjoining what is right, forbidding what is wrong, and believing in Allah" (Q.3:110). He should have to pray daily prayers whatever possible to do. Doing only obligatory prayers at worksites is permissible provided one doesn't find time and facility to do all. It all depends on one's intentions (*niya't*). If there is will there is way. The Prophet was very particular about obligatory prayers. As for voluntary prayers, he observed some on regular basis (like *Sunna moaqquada*) and some, on irregular basis (*Sunna Ghair Moaqquada*).

Fasting, Zakat and Hajj normally do not present any difficulty in their observance.

Make it a note that complete observance of Sharia Law in matters relating to '*ibadat*'(prayers) and '*mu'amlat*' (interactions among fellow beings) are enjoined in a true Islamic society where all believers have full opportunity and rights in the social and political setup to shape their life according to *Shari'a*. This was true with early Muslims, though in minority, were living in non-Muslim majority countries. But this is not true today even in most of the Muslim countries, not to speak of non-Muslim countries.

73. Can a Muslim use toilet paper for cleaning oneself after urination and toilet? What are the rules relating cleaning after urination and bowel clearance??

Yes, cleaning oneself after urination and bowel clearance with toilet papers is permissible. But use of water after cleaning toilet with toilet paper is most recommended.

The following from Imam Ghazzali's 'Ihya Ulum-ud-Din' (Revival of Religious Learning) will help us understand the rules relating 'Purification of Body from Impurities':

"If one is pressed by calls of nature, he should go from the view of men and take shelter behind something... When entering a bathroom, he should advance his left leg first and right leg next and should not urinate while standing. Companion Omar said: While I was urinating standing, the Prophet told me: O Omar! Don't pass urine standing. Ibnul Mobarak said: There is no harm in urinating in a bathroom if urine goes out flowing. The Prophet said: Let nobody among you urinate in a bathroom and make ablution at the same place. Before sitting for urination, one should take pebbles with him.[33]

"The Prophet said: Let one who uses stones (for cleaning toilet) use odd numbers (say three stones). He should first use the stones to clean his orifice. He should then move to another place and perform the act of cleaning with water when available. The use of stones and water both are desirable. It is said that when God revealed the verse: "Therein are men who love purity and God loves the pure" (9:109), the Prophet asked the people of Qub'a: What is the purity for which God has praised you? They said: We are accustomed to use both stones and water after calls of nature."[34] Use of toilet paper and water, or vice versa, are thus permissible on the analogy of the above text.

74. How do Muslims view about pets, like cats and dogs?

There is no Qur'anic prohibition or condemnation of pets. Many Prophetic traditions emphasize treating animals kindly and not overworking or beating them.

Dogs in the Islamic world are typically not allowed inside the house. They are considered to be unclean. A frequently cited *hadith* records that the Prophet forbade dogs inside the house for reason of hygiene. "Whoever keeps a dog except for hunting or for guarding crops or cattle will lose one large measure of his reward each day." On the basis of this hadith some jurists argue that the keeping of dogs as pets can be classified as '*makruh*' rather than '*haram*'.

Cats, known for their cleanliness, lived in the household of the Prophet. He and some of his companions were well known for their kindness to cats. Abu Huraira, one of the companions, used to have a bunch of cats in his house and was addressed by the name of 'father of cats'.

With the advancement of veterinary medicines and animals cleaning products the hygienic reason of dogs being unclean is no more valid. Muslims, particularly those who were born in the United States and Europe are now having dogs in their houses as pets. Others believe that the prohibition of dogs inside the house recorded in the hadith remains applicable to every time and place.

75. Are Lottery, Raffle and games of chance permissible in Islam?

Islamic legislation allows some ways in which one person can take money of another. They include trade, employment, gifts and inheritance.

Lottery is a method of gambling and all gambling are forbidden in Islam. Its prohibition is described in the Qur'an in the same verse, which prohibits all intoxicants. An important principle in Islam is not to sell something which has no benefit to man. Lottery, and things similar to lottery, like raffles and scratch tickets have no value unless they are won. Hence it is not permissible in Islam to sell and buy such tickets.

However, since Europe and America are not based on Islamic principles, the Muslim community cannot have control over such gambling institutions. But the community can have the control not to participate in such types of games of luck and chances.

76. Please suggest how to live a life of piety in America. Many aspects of American culture and traditions contradict the teachings and traditions of Islam.

To live a clean life in America needs conviction and faith in the principles "to do what is good and beneficial and abstain from what is evil and harmful". It needs personal integrity of character, which comes from the faith in "complete surrender to the Will of God" and willingness to remain steadfast to the legacy of forefathers.

Faith (*iman*) is the foundation of the believer and *tauheed* (belief in the existence and unity of God) is the essence of this faith. Safeguarding of this faith and this *tauheed* is the primary objective of all the Islamic teachings and legislation. To keep oneself purified of all traces of *shirk* and remnants of error, a continuous war must be waged against all the ills and evils of the society which originate in man's ignorance and in misleading slogans of privacy, individual rights and freedom.

"In the body there is a piece of flesh such that if it is good, the whole body is good, while if it is corrupted the whole body is corrupted, and that is the heart."[35]

"Deeds are judged by their intentions, and everyone will be judged according to what he intended."[36]

There are two kinds of sins every Muslim youth must guard himself against; they are sins of commission and sins of omission. Doing something, which is forbidden, and not doing something that is obligatory is the root cause of all the evils of the society.

77. One of the problems, we in America face, is how to stay innocent and pure. There are temptations at every step and evils all around. Please advise how to live a life of piety and innocence?

Integrity of character is the key to resist and fight all the evils of the society we are living in. But this integrity does not come by itself. We have to achieve it; we have to earn it. How? By conviction and belief in good and evil and that the good deeds will take us at the height of human achievements and evil deeds will put us in the pit of plight and ignominy. It's foolish to know the fire burning oneself. Annals of past are full of human experiences of good and evil. We can take lessons from them.

There are two great temptations before us; sex and money. Abundant opportunity and rights of privacy ignite one's temptation very comfortably. Young Muslims living in America, Europe or Canada have to have a real 'jihad' to protect themselves from the evils of their society. This society has one advantage also. While there is opportunity to earn money, proper or improper, and have sex without obligation of marriage; there is also opportunity to shape one's life on honesty and piety. While this society is open for crime and corruption, it also helps one to shape his life without crime and corruption. Of course, the lifestyle of the two will be quite different. One cannot survive his life in third-world countries without crime and corruptions.

78. What to do when a Muslim girl asks permission of her parents to marry her Christian classmate?

Our family is in great agony since our college going daughter, age 19, asked our permission to marry her classmate, a Christian youth. We are Muslim migrants, but our two sons and one daughter are all born and brought up in the USA. We are at loss to decide. Please help.

Muslim men are allowed to marry women from 'People of the Book'. The Prophet (PUH) himself married woman from Christian and Jewish tribes, after death of his first wife. One Qur'anic text (5:5) addresses the issue and allows the Prophet the liberty to do so. Some of the women became Muslims; some did not. But this practice of the Prophet is considered as exception, not the rule to follow.

Marriage regulations in Islam revolve around concerns regarding the faith of the children who will result from the union. Marriage between a Muslim man and someone from a community not possessing a revelation is considered against Islamic Law. It is preferable for Muslim men to marry Muslim women. However, they are allowed to marry Christian or Jewish women, because they are "People of the Book", those who have divine revelations.

Muslim women must marry a Muslim or someone who converts to Islam. Otherwise, the marriage of a Muslim woman to a non-Muslim man would represent the potential loss of identity and religious heritage of the children from that union.

In the case under consideration, there is no harm in allowing the girl to marry her boyfriend provided he agrees to convert to Islam. It is advisable for the parents to respect the feelings of their children so far they are legitimate and do not go against the tradition of the family. Similar obligations be followed by the children to sacrifice their likes and dislikes for best interests of their family.

There are numerous instances in the medieval caliphates of Abbasids of Baghdad, Umayyads of Spain and Fatimids of Egypt when Muslims married non-Muslims and vice versa. The Moghal king of India, Akbar the Great, had married a Hindu princess from Rajput family who was the mother of his successor king, Jehangir. Although the precedents of these monarchs cannot be ruling for the Muslim Ummah, the traditions and practices of Muslim community had been different in different lands at different time. Even in our present age one can find numerous instances of inter-faith marriages in Lebanon, Palestine, Syria, and even in India where Muslims are in largest minority.

79. Boys and girls addicted to drugs and social crimes:
Our eldest son, a teen of 18, has fallen in bad
company of his high-schoolmates, who are addicted
to drugs, shoplifting, and things like that, which
we have little knowledge. We have tried to make
him understand the consequences of such behavior
without any success. We are not practicing Muslims.
We are thinking to revert back to our home country.
We are confused and unable to make any decision.
We have one girl, 5 years younger than him. Please
show us a way out of this crisis.

Most of the immigrant families living in the USA and Europe have been facing such problems with their children. Teen age is in itself an explosive age in the life of every person. Undesirable social environment adds fuel to the fire. We suggest the following steps may help in remedying the problems to some extent:

Home is the primal school for every child. Kids learn by seeing and following their parents or their elders in the family. Parents, who cannot afford day-care, should try to give some time every day with their children. If parents or elders in the family have the ethical and religious background and behavior, the children will automatically have a moral base in their behavior. We may not apply religion in our wholesale secular life of America. But we cannot exclude ethics and morality from our home life. Human societies have gone thru. a series of evolution from the very beginning of creation. Religion has always been the fountainhead of ethics and morality. The more we distance our kids from religion the more moral and ethical problems will we face.

The second step that can help solve our kid's problems is 'early marriage'. Parents should try, if feasible, to get their boys or girls married at an early age of 18 to 22.

If a family finds that they are living in a neighborhood, not suitable for their children, try to relocate in a suitable place. Change of surrounding environment will greatly help solve the problems in question. A neighborhood of moral and ethical laxity is the breeding ground for crimes and corruption.

80. Are watching movies on screen, TV, DVD, or CDs permissible or prohibited?

There were no such electronic technologies during the seventh century world. The art of stage drama of live persons was there, but not very common. Today movies are important tools of instructions and recreation. Their situation is like that of any other tool, which in itself is neutral and harmless, and any ruling concerning it will depend on how it is used.

Movies of TV, DVD or game CD may be regarded as permissible and good—in fact desirable—if the following conditions are met:

First the contents of movie must be free of violence, crime and sex—indeed, free from anything which is against the norms of Islamic belief, morals and manners. Muslims, youngsters or adults, should avoid watching programs of sexual sensuality, greed for money and glorifying crimes and corruption.

Second, The watching of movies should not prevent one from daily routine obligations and religious duties. One of the most important reasons mentioned in the Qur'an for the prohibition of drinking and gambling is that they keep people away from remembering Allah and from *salat* (prayer).

Third free mixing among men and women or boys and girls in movie theatres should be avoided to prevent any chance of sexual undertones and temptations in the darkened hall. It is preferable at such occasion to add company of some elders from the family. The following *Hadith* relates to such occasion:

"It is better for one of you to be pricked in the head with an iron pick than to touch a woman whom it is unlawful to touch."[37]

As regards boys and girls watching films at home on TV or DVD, it is advisable to watch in company of some family member.

81. Songs and music are indispensable part of life now a days. What does Islam say about it?

Islam does not forbid entertainments, which comfort the soul, please the heart, and refresh the mind. Singing with music is permissible provided it fulfills the above-mentioned purpose.

In order to create an atmosphere of joy and happiness, singing is recommended on festive occasions such as 'Eids and national festivals, weddings, birth of a child, etc.

'Aishah narrated that when a Makkan woman was married to an Ansari man, the Prophet (pbuh) asked:

"Aishah, did they have any entertainment? The Ansar are fond of entertainments."[38]

Aishah narrated that during the days of Mina, on the day of Eid al-Adha, two girls were with her, singing and playing on the hand drum. The Prophet (pbuh) was present in a corner, listening to them. Abu Bakr then entered and rebuked the girls, not seeing the Prophet. The Prophet (pbuh) uncovering his face, told him, "Let them be, Abu Bakr. These are the days of Eid."[39]

In his book, *'Ihya ulum al-deen',* Imam al-Ghazzali mentions the *ahadith* about the singing girls, the Abyssinians playing with spears in the Prophet's Mosque, the Prophet's encouraging them by saying, "Carry on, O Bani Arfidah," and asking his wife, Aishah, "Would you like to watch?" al-Ghazzali then says: "All these *ahadith* are reported by al-Bukhari and Muslim in the two *Sahihs*, and they clearly prove that singing and playing (sports) are not forbidden (*haram*).

It is reported that many companions of the Prophet (may Allah be pleased with them) as well as the second generation of Muslim scholars used to listen to singing and did not see anything wrong with it. As for the *ahadith*, which have been reported against singing, they are all weak and have been shown by researchers to be unsound. The jurist Abu Bakr al-Arabi says, "No sound hadith is available concerning the prohibition of singing," while Ibn Hazm says, "All that is reported on this subject is false and fabricated."[40]

There is unanimous agreement that if singing is done in conjunction with forbidden (*haram*) activities – for example, at a drinking party, or mixed with obscenity and sin – it is forbidden.

ENDNOTES

1 Reported by al-Tirmizi, Abu Dawood and Ibn-e-Majah.
2 Reported by Ahmed ibn-Hanbal in al-Musnad.
3 The Muslim Conduct of State by Dr. Muhammad Hamidullah; p.24.
4 Ibid…p.41.
5 Imam al-Shatibi's "Theory of the Higher Objectives and Intents of Islamic Law" by Ahmed al-Raysuni; Trans. Nancy Roberts; p.xi.
6 Reported by al-Hakim.
7 The Spirit of Islam: Syed Ameer Ali; p.113
8 The Muslim Observer, a weekly newspaper, Jan. 6-12, 2006
9 'www.legal-database.com'
10 www.legal-database.com
11 www.legal-database.com
12 The Lawful and the Prohibited in Islam: by Yusuf al-Qaradwi; p.62
13 Reported in Sahih Bukhari, Muslim and Ibn Maja.
14 What Everyone Needs to Know About ISLAM; by John Esposito; p.173.
15 Reported in Abu Dawood.
16 The Spirit of Islam: Syed Ameer Ali. Pp.254-257.
17 Methodology in Islam: by Dr. Fazlur Rahman; p.56
18 Reported by Ahmed ibn-Hanbal.
19 "Truth & Fiction in The Da Vinci Code": by Bart D. Herman p.137
20 Responses to 101 Questions on Islam; by John Renard; p.109.
21 The Spirit of Islam: Syed Amir Ali. P.274
22 Ibid. p.272-274.
23 Muslims and the West: by Karen Armstrong; p.181
24 The Spirit of Islam; Syed Ameer Ali; p.58.
25 Reported by al-Bukhari and others.
26 Reported by Abu Dawood and Ibn Majah.
27 Reported by Malik in al-*Muwatta*.
28 Reported by al-Bukhari and Muslim.
29 What Went Wrong; by Bernard Lewis; p.36
30 Muslims in the West: by Syed Abul Hasan Ali Nadwi; p. 128.
31 The Lawful and the Prohibited in Islam; Yusuf al-Qaradawi; p.169
32 Reported in Sahee al-Bukhari and Muslim.
33 Imam Ghazali's "Ihya Uloomud Din"; Vol.I, p.126; Eng.translation: Fazlul Karim, Darul Isha'at, Karachi.
34 Ibid: p.127.
35 Reported by al-Bukhari, Muslim and others; narrated in al-Tirmidhi.

[36] Ibid.

[37] Reported by al-Bayhaqi and al-Tabarani on sound authority.

[38] Reported by al-Bukhari.

[39] Reported by ibn-Majah.

[40] The Lawful and the Prohibited in Islam by Yusuf al-Qaradwi; p.302

ABOUT THE AUTHOR

The author is a resident scholar having a thirst and urge to know the remedy of the chronic malady of Muslim Ummah living in the West. A graduate in Islamic disciplines from Karachi University, Pakistan; he developed an urge of knowledge as Research Fellow in Islamic Research Institute of Pakistan and was associated with teaching faculty of couple of undergraduate colleges in Karachi. His association with the National Archives and National Library of Pakistan for pretty long time gave him considerable opportunity to study and research on national and international issues. Currently, he is living in Miami, Florida. He can be reached at e-mail: ihasanfaq@yahoo.com.

www.ingramcontent.com/pod-product-compliance
Lightning Source LLC
Chambersburg PA
CBHW061246280526
45784CB00002B/654